CO

SHAKESPEARE
ANTHOLOGY

HarperCollins*Publishers*

HarperCollins Publishers
P.O. Box, Glasgow G4 0NB

First published 1994

Reprint 10 9 8 7 6 5 4 3 2 1 0

© HarperCollins Publishers 1994

ISBN 0 00 470720 6

Printed in Great Britain by
HarperCollins Manufacturing, Glasgow

CONTENTS

Histories

Poems and Sonnets

THE LIFE AND TIMES OF
William Shakespeare

Very little indeed is known about Shakespeare's private life: the facts included here are almost the only indisputable ones. The dates given of Shakespeare's plays are those on which they were first produced.

1558	Queen Elizabeth crowned.	
1561	Francis Bacon born.	
1564	Christopher Marlowe born.	William Shakespeare born April 23.
1566		Shakespeare's brother, Gilbert, born.
1567	Mary, Queen of Scots, deposed. James VI (later James I of England) crowned King of Scotland.	
1572	Ben Jonson born. Lord Leicester's Company (of players) licensed; later called Lord Strange's, then the Lord Chamberlain's, and finally (under James) The King's Men.	

1573	John Donne born.	
1574	The Common Council of London directs that all plays and playhouses in London must be licensed.	
1576	James Burbage builds the first public playhouse, The Theatre, at Shoreditch, outside the walls of the City.	
1577	Francis Drake begins his voyage round the world (completed 1580).	
	Holinshed's *Chronicles of England, Scotland and Ireland* published (which Shakespeare used extensively).	
1582		Shakespeare married to Anne Hathaway.
1583	The Queen's Company founded by royal warrant.	Shakespeare's daughter, Susanna, born.
1585		Shakespeare's twins, Hamnet and Judith, born.

1587	Mary, Queen of Scots, beheaded.	
	Marlowe's *Tamburlaine (Part I)* first staged.	
1588	Defeat of the Spanish Armada.	
	Marlowe's *Tamburlaine (Part II)* first staged.	
1589	Marlowe's *Jew of Malta* and Kyd's *Spanish Tragedy* (one of the most popular plays of Elizabethan times).	
1590	Spenser's *Faerie Queene* (Books I-III) published.	
1592	Marlowe's *Doctor Faustus* and *Edward II* first staged.	*Titus Andronicus, Henry VI, Parts I, II and III Richard III.*
	Witchcraft trials in Scotland.	
	Robert Greene, a rival playwright, refers to Shakespeare as 'an upstart crow' and 'the only Shake-scene in a country'.	

1593	London theatres closed by the plague. Christopher Marlowe killed in a Deptford tavern.	*The Two Gentlemen of Verona* *The Comedy of Errors* *The Taming of the Shrew* *Love's Labour's Lost*
1594	Shakespeare's company becomes The Lord Chamberlain's Men.	*Romeo and Juliet*
1595	Raleigh's first expedition to Guiana. Last expedition of Drake and Hawkins (both died).	*Richard II* *A Midsummer Night's Dream*
1596	Spenser's *Faerie Queene (Books IV-VI)* published. James Burbage buys rooms at Blackfriars and begins to convert them into a theatre.	*King John* *The Merchant of Venice* Shakespeare's son, Hamnet, dies. Shakespeare's father is granted a coat of arms.
1597	James Burbage dies; his son Richard, an actor, turns the Blackfriars Theatre into a private playhouse.	
1598	Death of Philip II of Spain.	*Henry IV (Part II)* *Much Ado about Nothing*
1599	Death of Edmund Spenser.	*Henry V* *Julius Cæsar* *As You Like It*

	The Globe Theatre completed at Bankside by Richard and Cuthbert Burbage.	
1600	Fortune Theatre built at Cripplegate.	*The Merry Wives of Windsor* *Troilus and Cressida*
	East India Company founded for the extension of English trade and influence in the East.	
	The Children of the Chapel begin to use the hall at Blackfriars.	
1601		*Hamlet, Twelfth Night*
1602	Sir Thomas Bodley's library opened at Oxford.	
1603	Death of Queen Elizabeth I.	
	James I comes to the throne.	
	Shakespeare's company becomes The King's Men.	
	Raleigh tried, condemned and sent to the Tower.	
1604	Treaty of peace with Spain.	*Measure for Measure* *Othello, All's Well that Ends Well*

1605	The Gunpowder Plot: an attempt by a group of Catholics to blow up the Houses of Parliament.	
1606	Guy Fawkes and other plotters executed.	*Macbeth* *King Lear*
1607	Virginia, in America, colonized. A great frost in England. The Thames froze over.	*Antony and Cleopatra* *Timon of Athens* *Coriolanus* Shakespeare's daughter, Susanna, married to Dr John Hall.
1608	The company of the Children of the Chapel Royal (who had performed at Blackfriars for ten years) is disbanded. John Milton born. Notorious pirates executed in London.	Richard Burbage leases the Blackfriars Theatre to six of his fellow actors, including Shakespeare. *Pericles, Prince of Tyre*
1609		Shakespeare's *Sonnets* published.
1610	A great drought in England	*Cymbeline*
1611	Chapman completes translation of the *Iliad*, the story of Troy.	*A Winter's Tale* *The Tempest*

	Authorized version of Bible published.	
1612	Webster's *The White Devil* first staged.	Shakespeare's brother, Gilbert, dies.
1613	Globe Theatre burnt down during a performance of *Henry VIII* (the firing of small cannon set fire to the thatched roof).	*Henry VIII* Shakespeare buys a house at Blackfriars.
	Webster's *Duchess of Malfi* first staged.	
1614	Globe Theatre rebuilt.	
1616	Ben Jonson publishes his plays in one volume.	Shakespeare's daughter, Judith, marries Thomas Quiney.
	Raleigh released from the Tower in order to prepare an expedition to gold mines of Guiana.	Death of Shakespeare on his birthday, April 23.
1618	Raleigh returns to England and is executed on charge for which he was imprisoned in 1603.	
1623	Publication of the Folio editon of Shakespeare's plays.	Death of Anne Shakespeare (née Hathaway).

THE COMEDIES

All's Well that Ends Well

Written 1602-3
Time and place of action 16th-Century France and
Italy

*Helena, in love with Bertram, is granted him in
marriage as a reward for curing the King.
Bertram, who does not want to marry her, immediately abandons her after the wedding. He states
that he will only take her as his wife when she
has secured a prized ring from his finger and borne
him a child. Helena achieves this by the 'bed trick'
where she takes the place of Diana whom Bertram
has been trying to seduce.*

'Twere all one
That I should love a bright particular star
And think to wed it, he is so above me.
In his bright radiance and collateral light
Must I be comforted, not in his sphere [I.i]
Helena referring to Bertram who is her social superior

Our remedies oft in ourselves do lie,
Which we ascribe to heaven. [I.i]
*Helena musing over how she can secure Bertram as her
husband*

Then shalt thou give me with thy kingly hand
What husband in thy power I will command.
Exempted be from me the arrogance
To choose from forth the royal blood of France,
My low and humble name to propagate
With any branch or image of thy state;
But such a one, thy vassal, whom I know
Is free for me to ask, thee to bestow. [II.i]
*Helena asking the King of France that she might choose a
husband as a reward for curing him*

But follows it, my lord, to bring me down
Must answer for your raising? I know her well:
She had her breeding at my father's charge.
A poor physician's daughter my wife! Disdain
Rather corrupt me ever! [II.iii]
*Bertram to the King of France, objecting that he should
have to marry beneath him*

If she, my liege, can make me know this clearly,
I'll love her dearly, ever, ever dearly [V.iii]
*Bertram, on finding out how Helena became pregnant
and obtained his ring*

As You Like It

Written 1599-1600
Time and place of action a Renaissance court and
  a forest setting

*Orlando and Rosalind fall in love. She, the daugh-
ter of the banished Duke, is in turn banished to
the Forest of Arden, accompanied by her cousin
Celia and the jester Touchstone. Orlando has also
gone there to join forces with her father. When he
meets the disguised Rosalind he fails to recognise
her. Orlando's brother, Oliver, comes to kill
Orlando but is saved by him from a lion. He and
Celia fall in love. Rosalind reveals herself to
Orlando and the rightful Duke is restored to
power. All the lovers are united.*

Now, my co-mates and brothers in exile,
Hath not old custom made this life more sweet
Than that of painted pomp? Are not these woods
More free from peril than the envious court?
Here feel we not the penalty of Adam,
The seasons' difference; as the icy fang

And churlish chiding of the winter's wind,
Which when it bites and blows upon my body,
Even till I shrink with cold, I smile and say
'This is no flattery; these are counsellors
That feelingly persuade me what I am.'
Sweet are the uses of adversity;
Which, like the toad, ugly and venomous,
Wears yet a precious jewel in his head;
And this our life, exempt from public haunt,
Finds tongues in trees, books in the running brooks,
Sermons in stones, and good in everything. [II.i]
*The Duke talking to some of his exiled band about life in
the Forest of Arden as opposed to Court Life.*

O good old man, how well in thee appears
The constant service of the antique world,
When service sweat for duty, not for meed!
Thou art not for the fashion of these times,
Where none will sweat but for promotion,
And having that do choke their service up
Even with the having. [II.iii]
*Orlando praising the old servant Adam who wishes to
accompany him into the Forest of Arden*

Ay, now am I in Arden; the more fool I; when I was
at home I was in a better place; but travellers must
be content. [II.iv]
*Touchstone, having accompanied Rosalind and Celia to
the Forest of Arden*

Under the greenwood tree
Who loves to lie with me,
And turn his merry note
Unto the sweet bird's throat,
Come hither, come hither, come hither.
Here shall he see
No enemy
But winter and rough weather. [II.v]
Song

I can suck melancholy out of a song, as a weasel
sucks eggs. [II.v]
Jacques, lord attending on banished Duke, who revels in
melancholy

All the world's a stage,
And all the men and women merely players;
They have their exits and their entrances;
And one man in his time plays many parts,
His acts being seven ages. At first the infant,
Mewling and puking in the nurse's arms;
Then the whining school-boy, with his satchel
And shining morning face, creeping like snail
Unwillingly to school. And then the lover,
Sighing like furnace, with a woeful ballad
Made to his mistress' eyebrow. Then a soldier,
Full of strange oaths, and bearded like the pard,
Jealous in honour, sudden and quick in quarrel,

17

Seeking the bubble reputation
Even in the cannon's mouth. And then the justice,
In fair round belly with good capon lin'd,
With eyes severe and beard of formal cut,
Full of wise saws and modern instances;
And so he plays his part. The sixth age shifts
Into the lean and slipper'd pantaloon,
With spectacles on nose and pouch on side,
His youthful hose, well sav'd, a world too wide
For his shrunk shank; and his big manly voice,
Turning again toward childish treble, pipes
And whistles in his sound. Last scene of all,
That ends this strange eventful history,
Is second childishness and mere oblivion;
Sans teeth, sans eyes, sans taste, sans every thing.
[II.vii]
Jacques philosophizing on the seven ages of man

A lean cheek, which you have not; a blue eye and
sunken, which you have not; an unquestionable
spirit, which you have not; a beard neglected, which
you have not; but I pardon you for that, for simply
your having in beard is a younger brother's rev-
enue. Then your hose should be ungarter'd, your
bonnet unbanded, your sleeve unbutton'd, your
shoe untied, and every thing about you demonstrat-
ing a careless desolation. But you are no such man;

you are rather point-device in your accoutrements,
as loving yourself than seeming the lover of any
other. [III.ii]
*Rosalind, disguised as a man, telling Orlando why he
doesn't appear to be in love*

I would cure you, if you would but call me Rosalind,
and come every day to my cote and woo me. [III.ii]
*Rosalind, disguised as a man, telling Orlando how she
can cure him of his love for Rosalind*

Men are April when they woo, December when
they wed: maids are May when they are maids, but
the sky changes when they are wives. I will be more
jealous of thee than a Barbary cock-pigeon over his
hen, more clamorous than a parrot against rain,
more new-fangled than an ape, more giddy in my
desires than a monkey. I will weep for nothing, like
Diana in the fountain, and I will do that when you
are disposed to be merry; I will laugh like a hyen,
and that when thou art inclin'd to sleep. [IV.i]
*Rosalind, disguised as a man, telling Orlando how mar-
riage affects men and women.*

Your brother and my sister no sooner met but they
look'd; no sooner look'd but they lov'd; no sooner
lov'd but they sigh'd; no sooner sigh'd but they
ask'd one another the reason; no sooner knew the

reason but they sought the remedy – and in these degrees have they made a pair of stairs to marriage, which they will climb incontinent, or else be incontinent before marriage. [V.ii]
Rosalind, disguised as a man, describing to Orlando how Oliver and Celia fell in love

Phebe: Good shepherd, tell this youth what 'tis to love.
Silvius: It is to be all made of sighs and tears ...
It is to be all made of faith and service ...
It is to be all made of fantasy,
All made of passion, and all made of wishes;
All adoration, duty, and observance,
All humbleness, all patience, and impatience;
All purity, all trial, all obedience. [V.ii]
Silvius describing love

I'll have no father, if you be not he;
I'll have no husband, if you be not he;
Nor ne'er wed woman, if you be not she. [V iv]
Rosalind, having revealed her identity, addressing her father, Orlando and Phebe (the shepherdess who had fallen in love with Rosalind disguised as a man)

The Comedy of Errors

Written Before 1594
Time and place of action 1st Century BC, Ephesus

Identical twin sons (both called Antipholus) and twin slaves (both called Dromio) are separated as babies following a shipwreck. The father of Antipolus, Ægeon, who is left with a son and a slave has also lost his wife Æmilia. At eighteen his son and slave go in search of their lost twins. After they have been gone for five years Ægeon goes to Ephesus in search of them. When he arrives he is seized and ordered to pay ransom on pain of death. Meanwhile his son and slave have arrived at Ephesus on the same day. The confusion occurs when they come across the long lost twin (now married) and the long lost slave. Eventually all is explained by an abbess who turns out to be Aegeon's long-lost wife, Æmilia.

There's nothing situate under heaven's eye
But hath his bound, in earth, in sea, in sky.
The beasts, the fishes, and the winged fowls,

Are their males' subjects, and at their controls.
Man, more divine, the master of all these,
Lord, of the wide world and wild watr'y seas,
Indu'd with intellectual sense and souls,
Of more pre-eminence than fish and fowls,
Are masters to their females, and their lords
Then let your will attend on their accords. [II.i]
*Luciana talking about male supremacy and how women
have to submit to it*

They brought one Pinch, a hungry lean-fac'd villain,
A mere anatomy, a mountebank,
A threadbare juggler, and a fortune-teller,
A needy, hollow-ey'd, sharp-looking wretch,
A living dead man. [V.i]
*A description of Pinch, the schoolmaster, who becomes
embroiled in the confusion*

Whoever bound him, I will loose his bonds,
And gain a husband by his liberty.
Speak, old Ægeon, if thou be'st the man
That hadst a wife once call'd Æmilia,
That bore thee at a burden two fair sons. [V.i]
*Æmilia, who had become an abbess in Ephesus, reveals
herself as Ægeon's long-lost wife and mother of the
twins, Antipholus*

Love's Labour's Lost

Written 1594-5
Time and place of action 16th-Century Navarre

The King of Navarre and three of his lords vow to
spend three years studying without female com-
panionship. The vows are soon broken when the
Princess of France and her ladies arrive on a
diplomatic mission. The King falls in love with
the Princess and his lords with her ladies, who do
not take them seriously. When the Princess's
father dies she and her ladies have to return home
hastily, they impose a year of probationary ser-
vice upon the King and his lords, promising to
marry them provided their love stands the test of
time and separation.

Let fame, that all hunt after in their lives,
Live regist'red upon our brazen tombs,
And then grace us in the disgrace of death;
When, spite of cormorant devouring Time,
Th' endeavour of this present breath may buy

That honour which shall bate his scythe's keen edge,
And make us heirs of all eternity. [I.i]
*The King urging his lords to spend three years studying
and without female company*

At Christmas I no more desire a rose
Than wish a snow in May's new-fangled shows;
But like of each thing that in season grows. [I.i]
*Berowne, one of the lords, warning the King against
undertaking something which is against their nature*

This wimpled, whining, purblind, wayward boy,
This senior-junior, giant-dwarf, Dan Cupid;
Regent of love rhymes, lord of folded arms,
Th' anointed sovereign of sighs and groans,
Liege of all loiterers and malcontents,
Dread prince of plackets, king of codpieces,
Sole imperator, and great general
Of trotting paritors. O my little heart!
And I to be a corporal of his field,
And wear his colours like a tumbler's hoop!
What? I! I love! I sue! I seek a wife!
A woman that is like a German clock,
Still a repairing; ever out of frame;
And never going aright, being a watch,
But being watch'd that it may still go right? [III.i]
*Berowne's humorous description of love to which he
admits having succumbed*

He hath never fed of the dainties that are bred in a
book; he hath not eat paper, as it were; he hath not
drunk ink; his intellect is not replenished; he is only
an animal, only sensible in the duller parts. [IV.ii]
Sir Nathaniel, the curate, who is scorning Dullard for his
lack of learning

Sweet lords, sweet lovers, O, let us embrace!
As true we are as flesh and blood can be.
The sea will ebb and flow, heaven show his face;
Young blood doth not obey an old decree.
We cannot cross the cause why we were born,
Therefore of all hands must we be forsworn. [IV.iii]
Berowne exhorting the King, Longaville and Dumain to
accept the fact that they have all succumbed to love

But love, first learned in a lady's eyes,
Lives not alone immured in the brain,
But with the motion of all elements
Courses as swift as thought in every power,
And gives to every power a double power,
Above their functions and their offices.
It adds a precious seeing to the eye:
A lover's eyes will gaze an eagle blind.
A lover's ear will hear the lowest sound,
When the suspicious head of theft is stopp'd.
Love's feeling is more soft and sensible
Than are the tender horns of cockled snails;

Love's tongue proves dainty Bacchus gross in taste.
For valour, is not Love a Hercules,
Still climbing trees in the Hesperides?
Subtle as Sphinx; as sweet and musical
As bright Apollo's lute, strung with his hair.
And when Love speaks, the voice of all the gods
Make heaven drowsy with the harmony.
Never durst poet touch a pen to write
Until his ink were temp'red with Love's sighs:
Oh, then his lines would ravish savage ears,
And plant in tyrants mild humility.
From women's eyes this doctrine I derive.
They sparkle still the right Promethean fire;
They are the books, the arts, the academes,
That show, contain, and nourish, all the world. [IV.iii]
Berowne talking of women and love and learning

Moth: They have been at a great feast of languages
and stol'n the scraps.
Costard: O, they have liv'd long on the alms-basket
of words. I marvel thy master hath not eaten thee
for a word, for thou art not so long by the head as
honorificabilitudinitatibus; thou art easier swallowed than a flap-dragon. [V.i]
*Moth and Costard making fun of the verbosity of Sir
Nathaniel and Holofernes*

The posteriors of this day; which the rude multitude
call the afternoon. [V.i]
*An example of Don Adriano de Armado's pompous turn
of phrase*

Taffeta phrases, silken terms precise,
Three-pil'd hyperboles, spruce affectation,
Figures pedantical – these summer-flies
Have blown me full of maggot ostentation.
I do forswear them; and I here protest,
By this white glove – how white the hand, God
knows! –
Henceforth my wooing mind shall be express'd
In russet yeas, and honest kersey noes.
And, to begin, wench – so God help me, law! –
My love to thee is sound, sans crack or flaw. [V.ii]
*Berowne promises Rosaline to give up his fancy words to
woo her*

A jest's prosperity lies in the ear
Of him that hears it, never in the tongue
Of him that makes it. [V.ii]
*Rosaline telling Berowne that he must soften his ironic
wit with sympathy by spending a year visiting hospitals
and making the ill laugh*

Measure for Measure

Written 1603-4
Time and place of action 16th-Century Vienna

Duke Vincentio entrusts the cleaning-up of Vienna to his puritanical deputy, Angelo, who invokes a forgotten law to condemn Claudio to death for getting Juliet pregnant. Claudio begs his sister, Isabella, to intercede for him. Angelo offers to spare Claudio in exchange for Isabella's virginity. Claudio pleads with Isabella to save his life. The Duke, disguised as a friar, persuades her to agree to the 'bed trick', with Mariana, Angelo's former betrothed, taking Isabella's place; nonetheless Angelo orders Claudio's execution which is prevented by another trick. No longer in disguise, the Duke decrees that Claudio and Juliet should marry, and so should Angelo and Mariana. He declares his own love for Isabella.

Now, as fond fathers,
Having bound up the threat'ning twigs of birch,
Only to stick it in their children's sight

For terror, not to use, in time the rod
Becomes more mock'd than fear'd; so our decrees,
Dead to infliction, to themselves are dead;
And liberty plucks justice by the nose;
The baby beats the nurse, and quite athwart
Goes all decorum. [I.iii]
*The Duke realises that his administration of his dukedom
has been too lax and he wants to remedy the situation*

A man whose blood
Is very snow-broth, one who never feels
The wanton stings and motions of the sense,
But doth rebate and blunt his natural edge
With profits of the mind, study and fast. [I.iv]
Lucio describing Angelo

We must not make a scarecrow of the law,
Setting it up to fear the birds of prey,
And let it keep one shape till custom make it
Their perch, and not their terror. [II.i]
Angelo telling Escalus about his plans for enforcing laws

'Tis one thing to be tempted, Escalus,
Another thing to fall. I not deny
The jury, passing on the prisoner's life,
May in the sworn twelve have a thief or two
Guiltier than him they try: what's open made to
Justice,

That justice seizes. What know the laws,
That thieves do pass on thieves? 'Tis very pregnant,
The jewel that we find, we stoop and take 't
Because we see it; but what we do not see,
We tread upon, and never think of it. [II.i]
*Angelo telling Escalus that the faults of others are no
justification for our own faults*

Well, Heaven forgive him! and forgive us all!
Some rise by sin, and some by virtue fall;
Some run from breaks of ice, and answer none,
and some condemned for a fault alone. [II.i]
*Escalus, commenting on Angelo's implacable decision to
execute Claudio*

Condemn the fault and not the actor of it! [II.ii]
Angelo's response to Isabella's plea to spare her brother

No ceremony that to great ones longs,
Not the king's crown nor the deputed sword,
The marshal's truncheon nor the judge's robe,
Become them with one half so good a grace
As mercy does. [II.ii]
Isabella pleads with Angelo to show mercy to her brother

The law hath not been dead, though it hath slept. [II.ii]
*The laws have been lax but Angelo is determined to have
them enforced*

O, it is excellent
To have a giant's strength! But it is tyrannous
To use it like a giant. [II.ii]
Isabella continues to plead for her brother's life

Man, proud man,
Dress'd in a little brief authority,
Most ignorant of what he's most assur'd,
His glassy essence, like an angry ape,
Plays such fantastic tricks before high heaven
As makes the angels weep. [II.ii]
Isabella condemning Angelo for his implacable authority

Great men may jest with saints: 'tis wit in them;
But in the less, foul profanation...
That in the captain's but a choleric word
Which in the soldier is flat blasphemy. [II.ii]
Isabella on the privilege of authority

O cunning enemy, that, to catch a saint,
With saints dost bait thy hook! Most dangerous
Is that temptation that doth goad us on
To sin in loving virtue. Never could the strumpet,
With all her double vigour, art and nature,
Once stir my temper; but this virtuous maid
Subdues me quite. Ever till now
When men were fond, I smil'd and wond'red. [II.ii]
Angelo realises his attraction to the virtuous Isabella

Which had you rather – that the most just law
Now took your brother's life; or, to redeem him,
Give up your body to such sweet uncleanness
As she that he hath stain'd? [II.iv]
*Angelo tells Isabella he will show her brother mercy if she
becomes his lover*

Better it were a brother died at once
Than that a sister, by redeeming him,
Should die for ever. [II iv]
*Isabella is not prepared to suffer eternal damnation by
sleeping with Angelo in order to save her brother*

Claudio: The miserable have no other medicine
But only hope:
I have hope to live, and am prepar'd to die.
Duke: Be absolute for death; either death or life
Shall thereby be the sweeter. Reason thus with life.
If I do lose thee, I do lose a thing
That none but fools would keep. A breath thou art,
Servile to all the skyey influences,
That dost this habitation where thou keep'st,
Hourly afflict. Merely, thou art Death's fool;
For him thou labour'st by thy flight to shun
And yet run'st toward him still. [III.i]
*The Duke, disguised as a friar, consoles Claudio on his
impending fate and the vanity of life*

Dar'st thou die?
The sense of death is most in apprehension;
And the poor beetle that we tread upon
In corporal sufferance finds a pang as great
As when a giant dies. [III.i]
Isabella tries to comfort Claudio on his impending death

Claudio: Death is a fearful thing.
Isabella: And shamed life a hateful.
Claudio: Ay, but to die, and go we know not where;
To lie in cold obstruction, and to rot;
This sensible warm motion to become
A kneaded clod; and the delighted spirit
To bathe in fiery floods or to reside
In thrilling region of thick-ribbed ice;
To be imprison'd in the viewless winds,
And blown with restless violence round about
The pendent world; or to be worse than worst
Of those that lawless and incertain thought
Imagine howling – 'tis too horrible.
The weariest and most loathed worldly life
That age, ache, penury, and imprisonment,
Can lay on nature is a paradise
To what we fear of death. [III.i]
Claudio describes the terrors of death

Some report a sea-maid spawn'd him; some, that he
was begot between two stock-fishes. But it is certain
that when he makes water his urine is congeal'd ice.
[III.ii]
Luicio describing Angelo

O, your desert speaks loud; and I should wrong it
To lock it in the wards of covert bosom,
When it deserves, with characters of brass,
A forted residence 'gainst the tooth of time
And razure of oblivion. [V.i]
The Duke addressing Angelo on his 'return' to Vienna

The very mercy of the law cries out
Most audible, even from his proper tongue,
'An Angelo for Claudio, death for death!'
Haste still pays haste, and leisure answers leisure;
Like doth quit like, and Measure still for Measure.
[V.i]
*The Duke exposes Angelo for his violation of Mariana
(whom he believed to be Isabella) and for breaking his
promise of redeeming Claudio*

They say best men are moulded out of faults;
And, for the most, become much more the better
For being a little bad; so may my husband. [V.i]
*Mariana appeals to the Duke to pardon her husband
Angelo*

The Merchant of Venice

Written 1596-7
Time and place of action Renaissance Venice and
  Belmont

*Bassanio asks his merchant friend Antonio to
lend him money to woo Portia. Antonio borrows
from Shylock, a Jewish moneylender who hates
him, agreeing to a bond giving Shylock a pound of
Antonio's flesh if the moneylender is not repaid
within three months. As Bassanio and Portia
announce their betrothal, news comes that
Antonio's ships have foundered and Shylock is
demanding his due. At the trial, Portia, disguised
as a lawyer, successfully defends Antonio by
showing that the bond gives Shylock only flesh,
not blood. The Duke pardons Shylock on condition that he become a Christian and share his
money with his daughter, Jessica, who has eloped
with the Christian Lorenzo.*

Antonio: In sooth, I know not why I am so sad.
It wearies me; you say it wearies you;
But how I caught it, found it, or came by it,
What stuff 'tis made of, whereof it is born,
I am to learn;
And such a want-wit sadness makes of me
That I have much ado to know myself.
Salerio: Your mind is tossing on the ocean;
There where your argosies, with portly sail –
Like signiors and rich burghers on the flood,
Or as it were the pageants of the sea –
Do overpeer the petty traffickers,
That curtsy to them, do them reverence,
As they fly by them with their woven wings.
[I.i]
Antonio is sad and his friend Salerio thinks he might be worrying about his investments on ships

Gratiano: You look not well, Signior Antonio;
You have too much respect upon the world;
They lose it that do buy it with much care....
*Antonio:*I hold the world but as the world, Gratiano –
A stage, where every man must play a part,
And mine a sad one. [I.i]
Gratiano warns Antonio of worrying too much about worldly things

Let me play the fool.
With mirth and laughter let old wrinkles come;
And let my liver rather heat with wine
Than my heart cool with mortifying groans.
Why should a man whose blood is warm within
Sit like his grandsire cut in alabaster?
Sleep when he wakes, and creep into the jaundice
By being peevish? [I.i]
Gratiano, on how cheerfulness is so much better than
melancholy

Fish not with this melancholy bait
For this fool gudgeon, this opinion. [I.i]
Gratiano warns Antonio against affecting a melancholy
aspect

Gratiano speaks an infinite deal of nothing, more
than any man in all Venice. His reasons are as two
grains of wheat hid in two bushels of chaff: you
shall seek all day ere you find them, and when you
have them they are not worth the search. [I.i]
Bassanio says that Gratiano speaks too much

In Belmont is a lady richly left,
And she is fair and, fairer than that word,
Of wondrous virtues. Sometimes from her eyes
I did receive fair speechless messages. [I.i]
Bassanio describes Portia

They are as sick that surfeit with too much as they that starve with nothing. It is no mean happiness, therefore, to be seated in the mean: superfluity comes sooner by white hairs, but competency lives longer. [I.ii]
Nerissa, Portia's maid, claims that happiness is having neither too much nor too little – the golden mean

If to do were as easy as to know what were good to do, chapels had been churches, and poor men's cottages princes' palaces. It is a good divine that follows his own instructions; I can easier teach twenty what were good to be done than be one of the twenty to follow mine own teaching. [I.ii]
Portia says it is all very well knowing what is right, it is so much more difficult to do it

I think he bought his doublet in Italy, his round hose in France, his bonnet in Germany, and his behaviour everywhere. [I.ii]
Portia and Nerissa making fun of one of Portia's suitors, Falconbridge

I will buy with you, sell with you, talk with you, walk with you, and so following; but I will not eat with you, drink with you, nor pray with you. [I.iii]
Shylock tells Bassanio he is only prepared to conduct business with him, nothing else

How like a fawning publican he looks!
I hate him for he is a Christian;
But more for that in low simplicity
He lends out money gratis, and brings down
The rate of usance here with us in Venice.
If I can catch him once upon the hip,
I will feed fat the ancient grudge I bear him.
He hates our sacred nation and he rails,
Even there where merchants most do congregate,
On me, my bargains, and my well-won thrift,
Which he calls interest. [I.iii]
Shylock on how much he hates Antonio

The devil can cite Scripture for his purpose.
An evil soul producing holy witness
Is like a villain with a smiling cheek,
A goodly apple rotten at the heart.
O, what a goodly outside falsehood hath! [I.iii]
Antonio warns Bassanio of hypocrisy in Shylock

Signior Antonio, many a time and oft
In the Rialto you have rated me
About my moneys and my usances;
Still have I borne it with a patient shrug,
For suff'rance is the badge of all our tribe;
You call me misbeliever, cut-throat dog,
And spit upon my Jewish gaberdine,
And all for use of that which is mine own. [I.iii]
Shylock recalls Antonio's treatment of him

You that did void your rheum upon my beard
And foot me as you spurn a stranger cur
Over your threshold; moneys is your suit.
What should I say to you? Should I not say
'Hath a dog money? Is it possible
A cur can lend three thousand ducats?' Or
Shall I bend low and, in a bondman's key,
With bated breath and whisp'ring humbleness,
Say this:
'Fair sir, you spit on me Wednesday last,
You spurn'd me such a day; another time
You call'd me dog; and for these courtesies
I'll lend you thus much moneys'? [I.iii]
Shylock asks why he should lend Antonio money

Love is blind, and lovers cannot see
The pretty follies that themselves commit.
For, if they could, Cupid himself would blush
To see me thus transformed to a boy [II.vi]
*Jessica and Lorenzo are eloping. She is ashamed of her
disguise as a boy*

Men that hazard all
Do it in hope of fair advantages.
A golden mind stoops not to shows of dross. [II.vii]
*The Prince of Morocco rejects the lead casket in favour of
the gold*

'All that glisters is not gold,
Often have you heard that told.
Many a man his life hath sold
But my outside to behold.
Gilded tombs do worms enfold.
Had you been as wise as bold,
Young in limbs, in judgment old,
Your answer had not been inscroll'd.
Fare you well, your suit is cold.' [II.vii]
The message inside the golden casket

What many men desire, that 'many' may be meant
By the fool multitude, that choose by show,
Not learning more than the fond eye doth teach;
Which pries not to th' interior, but, like the martlet,
Builds in the weather on the outward wall,
Even in the force and road of casualty.
I will not choose what many men desire,
Because I will not jump with common spirits
And rank me with the barbarous multitudes. [II.ix]
The Prince of Arragon choosing the silver casket

Hath not a Jew eyes? Hath not a Jew hands, organs,
dimensions, senses, affections, passions, fed with
the same food, hurt with the same weapons, subject
to the same diseases, healed by the same means,
warmed and cooled by the same winter and summer, as a Christian is? If you prick us, do we not
bleed? If you tickle us, do we not laugh? If you poi-

son us, do we not die? And if you wrong us, shall
we not revenge? If we are like you in the rest, we
will resemble you in that. [III.i]
Shylock wants revenge

Tell me where is fancy bred,
Or in the heart or in the head,
How begot, how nourished?
    Reply, reply.
It is engend'red in the eyes,
With gazing fed; and fancy dies
In the cradle where it lies.
Let us all ring fancy's knell:
I'll begin it – Ding, dong, bell. [III.ii]
A song sung to Bassanio while making his choice of casket

So may the outward shows be least themselves;
The world is still deceiv'd with ornament.
In law, what plea so tainted and corrupt
But, being season'd with a gracious voice,
Obscures the show of evil? In religion,
What damned error but some sober brow
Will bless it, and approve it with a text,
Hiding the grossness with fair ornament?
There is no vice so simple but assumes
Some mark of virtue on his outward parts. [III.ii]
*Bassanio musing over which casket to choose is wary of
outward appearance*

You'll ask me why I rather choose to have
A weight of carrion flesh than to receive
Three thousand ducats. I'll not answer that,
But say it is my humour – is it answer'd?
What if my house be troubled with a rat,
And I be pleas'd to give ten thousand ducats
To have it ban'd? What, are you answer'd yet?
Some men there are love not a gaping pig;
Some that are mad if they behold a cat;
And others, when the bagpipe sings i' th' nose,
Cannot contain their urine. [IV.i]
Shylock's reason for revenge

The pound of flesh which I demand of him
Is dearly bought, 'tis mine, and I will have it. [IV.i]
Shylock is determined to get his pound of flesh

Portia: Then must the Jew be merciful.
Shylock: On what compulsion must I? Tell me that.
Portia: The quality of mercy is not strain'd;
It droppeth as the gentle rain from heaven
Upon the place beneath. It is twice bless'd:
It blesseth him that gives and him that takes.
'Tis mightiest in the mightiest; it becomes
The throned monarch better than his crown;
His sceptre shows the force of temporal power,
The attribute to awe and majesty,
Wherein doth sit the dread and fear of kings;

But mercy is above the sceptred sway,
It is enthroned in the hearts of kings,
It is an attribute to God himself;
And earthly power doth then show likest God's
When mercy seasons justice. Therefore, Jew,
Though justice be thy plea, consider this –
That in the course of justice none of us
Should see salvation; we do pray for mercy,
And that same prayer doth teach us all to render
The deeds of mercy. [IV.i]
Portia disguised as a lawyer argues for clemency

Nay, take my life and all, pardon not that.
You take my house when you do take the prop
That doth sustain my house; you take my life
When you do take the means whereby I live. [IV.i]
*Shylock's response to having all his wealth confiscated –
they might as well execute him*

How sweet the moonlight sleeps upon this bank!
Here will we sit and let the sounds of music
Creep in our ears; soft stillness and the night
Become the touches of sweet harmony.
Sit, Jessica. Look, how the floor of heaven
Is thick inlaid with patines of bright gold;
There's not the smallest orb which thou behold'st
But in his motion like an angel sings,
Still quiring to the young-ey'd cherubins;
Such harmony is in immortal souls,

But whilst this muddy vesture of decay
Doth grossly close it in, we cannot hear it. [V.i]
*Jessica, Shylock's daughter, and Lorenzo enjoying the
moonlight*

The man that hath no music in himself,
Nor is not mov'd with concord of sweet sounds,
Is fit for treasons, stratagems, and spoils;
The motions of his spirit are dull as night,
And his affections dark as Erebus.
Let no such man be trusted. [V.i]
Lorenzo on his philosophy of music

The crow doth sing as sweetly as the lark
When neither is attended; and I think
The nightingale, if she should sing by day,
When every goose is cackling, would be thought
No better a musician than the wren.
How many things by season season'd are
To their right praise and true perfection! [V.i]
*Portia to Nerissa saying that things are only good within
their season*

Let me give light, but let me not be light,
For a light wife doth make a heavy husband. [V.i]
Portia to Bassanio

The Merry Wives of Windsor

Written 1597-8
Time and place of action Medieval Windsor

Falstaff, the jovial character from Henry IV, comes to Windsor. He amuses himself by pursuing the wives of two merchants. He writes them both identical love letters but they get wind of his intentions and between them they contrive to have him beaten up as a witch and also dumped into the Thames from a laundry basket. Falstaff, not deterred, is eventually exposed by the two wives in Windsor Forest at night, to the amusement of all the onlookers. Meanwhile, Anne, the daughter of one of the two wives, Mistress Ford, is being courted by three men. She eventually runs off with the one she loves and marries him.

I do mean to make love to Ford's wife; I spy entertainment in her; she discourses, she carves, she gives the leer of invitation. [I.iii]
Falstaff telling Nym and Pistol of his intentions to pursue Mistress Ford who he thinks fancies him

I have writ me here a letter to her; and here another
to Page's wife, who even now gave me good eyes
too, examin'd my parts with most judicious oeil-
lades; sometimes the beam of her view gilded my
foot, sometimes my portly belly. [I.iii]
*Falstaff telling Nym and Pistol how Mistress Page also
fancies him. He has written to both women*

I will be cheaters to them both, and they shall be
exchequers to me; they shall be my East and West
Indies, and I will trade to them both. [I.iii]
Falstaff's intentions with the two wives

What tempest, I trow, threw this whale, with so
many tuns of oil in his belly, ashore at Windsor? [II.i]
*Mistress Ford bemoans the fact that Falstaff is in
Windsor and has the audacity to pursue her*

I warrant he hath a thousand of these letters, writ
with blank space for different names – sure more! –
and these are of the second edition. [II.i]
Mistresses Page and Ford have received the same letter

Have I liv'd to be carried in a basket, like a barrow
of butcher's offal, and to be thrown in the Thames?
Well, if I be serv'd such another trick, I'll have my
brains ta'en out and butter'd, and give them to a
dog for a new-year's gift. The rogues slighted me
into the river with as little remorse as they would

have drown'd a blind bitch's puppies, fifteen i' th'
litter; and you may know by my size that I have a
kind of alacrity in sinking; if the bottom were as
deep as hell I should down. I had been drown'd but
that the shore was shelvy and shallow – a death that
I abhor; for the water swells a man; and what a
thing should I have been when I had been swell'd! I
should have been a mountain of mummy. [III.v]
*Falstaff recalling with indignation how he had been
dumped into the Thames*

Fie on sinful fantasy!
Fie on lust and luxury!
Lust is but a bloody fire,
Kindled with unchaste desire,
Fed in heart, whose flames aspire,
As thoughts do blow them, higher and higher.
Pinch him, fairies, mutually;
Pinch him for his villainy;
Pinch him and burn him and turn him about,
Till candles and star-light and moonshine be out. [V.v]
*The citizens of Windsor disguised as fairies and hobgob-
lins pinch Falstaff in the forest*

Let us every one go home,
And laugh this sport o'er by a country fire;
Sir John and all. [V.v]
*Mistress Page invites everyone, including Falstaff, home.
There are no bad feelings*

A Midsummer Night's Dream

Written 1595-6
Time and place of action Antiquity, Athens and the wood nearby

In a wood near Athens, some local workmen are rehearsing a play to celebrate Duke Theseus's impending marriage. The eloping lovers, Hermia and Lysander, go to the wood, followed by Demetrius who is in love with Hermia, and by Helena who is in love with Demetrius. Oberon, the Fairy King, has quarrelled with his consort Titania, and enchants her so that she falls in love with the first creature that she sees on waking. This is Bottom, the weaver, given an ass's head by the mischievous Puck. The four lovers also fall into a tangle of enchantment and confusion until Oberon lifts the spells. Titania thinks she has dreamt of her infatuation with Bottom. The play of Pyramus and Thisby is performed in honour of a triple wedding, since Demetrius has ended up with Helena.

Question your desires,
Know of your youth, examine well your blood,
Whether, if you yield not to your father's choice,
You can endure the livery of a nun,
For aye to be in shady cloister mew'd,
To live a barren sister all your life,
Chanting faint hymns to the cold fruitless moon.
Thrice-blessed they that master so their blood
To undergo such maiden pilgrimage;
But earthlier happy is the rose distill'd
Than that which withering on the virgin thorn
Grows, lives, and dies, in single blessedness. [I.i]
Theseus, Duke of Athens, asks Hermia to consider
whether she would prefer to spend her life in a nunnery
than wed the man her father has chosen for her

Ay me! for aught that I could ever read,
Could ever hear by tale or history,
The course of true love never did run smooth. [I.i]
Lysander laments to Hermia about their unlucky situation

O, teach me how you look, and with what art
You sway the motion of Demetrius' heart! [I.i]
Helena wants Hermia to tell her how she can get
Demetrius to fall in love with her rather than Hermia

How happy some o'er other some can be!
Through Athens I am thought as fair as she.

But what of that? Demetrius thinks not so;
He will not know what all but he do know.
And as he errs, doting on Hermia's eyes,
So I, admiring of his qualities.
Things base and vile, holding no quantity,
Love can transpose to form and dignity.
Love looks not with the eyes, but with the mind;
And therefore is wing'd Cupid painted blind. [I.i]
*Helena, on her unhappy situation regarding love and
Demetrius*

The most Lamentable Comedy, and most Cruel
Death of Pyramus and Thisby. [I.ii]
*The play that Quince, Snug, Bottom, etc. are going to
perform at the Duke's wedding*

I could play Ercles rarely, or a part to tear a cat in, to
make all split. [I.ii]
Bottom on his acting skills

I will roar that I will do any man's heart good to
hear me; I will roar that I will make the Duke say
'Let him roar again, let him roar again'. [I.ii]
Bottom wants to play the lion as well

Puck: How now, spirit! whither wander you?
Fairy: Over hill, over dale,
Thorough bush, thorough brier,

Over park, over pale,
Thorough flood, thorough fire,
I do wander every where,
Swifter than the moon's sphere;
And I serve the Fairy Queen,
To dew her orbs upon the green.
The cowslips tall her pensioners be;
In their gold coats spots you see;
Those be rubies, fairy favours,
In those freckles live their savours.
I must go seek some dewdrops here,
And hang a pearl in every cowslip's ear. [II.i]
The fairy meeting Puck

I am that merry wanderer of the night.
I jest to Oberon, and make him smile
When I a fat and bean-fed horse beguile,
Neighing in likeness of a filly foal;
And sometime lurk I in a gossip's bowl
In the very likeness of a roasted crab,
And, when she drinks, against her lips I bob,
And on her withered dewlap pour the ale.
The wisest aunt, telling the saddest tale,
Sometime for three-foot stool mistaketh me;
Then slip I from her bum, down topples she,
And 'tailor' cries, and falls into a cough;
And then the whole quire hold their hips and laugh,

And waxen in their mirth, and neeze, and swear
A merrier hour was never wasted there. [II.i]
Puck telling the fairy about his deeds

Therefore the moon, the governess of floods,
Pale in her anger, washes all the air,
That rheumatic diseases do abound.
And thorough this distemperature we see
The seasons alter: hoary-headed frosts
Fall in the fresh lap of the crimson rose. [II.i]
*Titania speaking of the discord in the fairy kingdom and
how it affects the world*

But I might see young Cupid's fiery shaft
Quench'd in the chaste beams of the wat'ry moon;
And the imperial votress passed on,
In maiden mediation, fancy-free.
Yet mark'd I where the bolt of Cupid fell.
It fell upon a little western flower,
Before milk-white, now purple with love's wound,
And maidens call it Love-in-idleness. [II.i]
*Oberon, King of the Fairies, asks Puck to go in search of a
flower which Cupid has steeped in love. Oberon will use
it to cast a spell on Titania*

I know a bank where the wild thyme blows,
Where oxlips and the nodding violet grows,
Quite over-canopied with luscious woodbine,

With sweet musk-roses, and with eglantine;
There sleeps Titania sometime of the night,
Lull'd in these flowers with dances and delight;
And there the snake throws her enamell'd skin,
Weed wide enough to wrap a fairy in. [II.i]
Oberon tells Puck where he can find Titania to apply the
magic love flower to her eyes

What hempen homespuns have we swagg'ring here,
So near the cradle of the Fairy Queen?
What, a play toward! I'll be an auditor ;
An actor too perhaps, if I see cause. [III.i]
Puck comes across the actors near the sleepingTitania

Bless thee, Bottom, bless thee! Thou art translated.
[III.i]
Puck, to make mischief, has given Bottom an ass's head

My mistress with a monster is in love.
Near to her close and consecrated bower,
While she was in her dull and sleeping hour,
A crew of patches, rude mechanicals,
That work for bread upon Athenian stalls,
Were met together to rehearse a play
Intended for great Theseus' nuptial day.
The shallowest thickskin of that barren sort,
Who Pyramus presented, in their sport
Forsook his scene and ent'red in a brake;

When I did him at this advantage take,
An ass's nole I fixed on his head.
Anon his Thisby must be answered,
And forth my mimic comes. When they him spy,
As wild geese that the creeping fowler eye,
Or russet-pated choughs, many in sort,
Rising and cawing at the gun's report,
Sever themselves and madly sweep the sky,
So at his sight away his fellows fly;
And at our stamp here, o'er and o'er one falls;
He murder cries, and help from Athens calls.
Their sense thus weak, lost with their fears thus strong,
Made senseless things begin to do them wrong,
For briers and thorns at their apparel snatch;
Some sleeves, some hats, from yielders all things catch.
I led them on in this distracted fear,
And left sweet Pyramus translated there;
When in that moment, so it came to pass,
Titania wak'd, and straightway lov'd an ass.
[III.ii]
*Puck recounting to Oberon how he had given Bottom an
ass's head which sent the players scattering in fear.
Titania woke, saw Bottom and fell in love*

Lord, what fools these mortals be! [III.ii]
Puck, on the mix-up of lovers

Is all the counsel that we two have shar'd,
The sisters' vows, the hours that we have spent,
When we have chid the hasty-footed time
For parting us – O, is all forgot?
All school-days' friendship, childhood innocence?
We, Hermia, like two artificial gods,
Have with our needles created both one flower,
Both on one sampler, sitting on one cushion,
Both warbling of one song, both in one key;
As if our hands, our sides, voices, and minds,
Had been incorporate. So we grew together,
Like to a double cherry, seeming parted,
But yet an union in partition,
Two lovely berries moulded on one stem;
So, with two seeming bodies, but one heart;
Two of the first, like coats in heraldry,
Due but to one, and crowned with one crest.
And will you rent our ancient love asunder,
To join with men in scorning your poor friend?
It is not friendly, 'tis not maidenly;
Our sex, as well as I, may chide you for it,
Though I alone do feel the injury. [III.ii]
*Helena is hurt that her great friend Hermia is making
fun of her with the men*

Ay, do – persever, counterfeit sad looks,
Make mouths upon me when I turn my back. [III.ii]
Helena is hurt that they are making fun of her

Jack shall have Jill;
Nought shall go ill;
The man shall have his mare again, and all shall be
well. [III.ii]
Puck will put things right

I must to the barber's, mounsieur; for methinks I am
marvellous hairy about the face. [IV.i]
Bottom talking to Titania

Methinks I have a great desire to a bottle of hay.
Good hay, sweet hay, hath no fellow. [IV.i]
What Bottom wants to eat (or drink)

My Oberon! What visions have I seen!
Methought I was enamour'd of an ass. [IV.i]
*Titania believes she has dreamt of her infatuation with
Bottom*

The eye of man hath not heard, the ear of man hath
not seen, man's hand is not able to taste, his tongue
to conceive, nor his heart to report, what my dream
was. [IV.i]
*Bottom says his dream was too strange for anyone to
believe*

The lunatic, the lover, and the poet,
Are of imagination all compact.

One sees more devils than vast hell can hold;
That is the madman. The lover, all as frantic,
Sees Helen's beauty in a brow of Egypt.
The poet's eye, in a fine frenzy rolling,
Doth glance from heaven to earth, from earth to
heaven;
And as imagination bodies forth
The forms of things unknown, the poet's pen
Turns them to shapes, and gives to airy nothing
A local habitation and a name.
Such tricks hath strong imagination
That, if it would but apprehend some joy,
It comprehends some bringer of that joy;
Or in the night, imagining some fear,
How easy is a bush suppos'd a bear? [V.i]
Theseus talks about the power of imagination

If we offend, it is with our good will.
That you should think, we come not to offend,
But with good will. To show our simple skill,
That is the true beginning of our end.
Consider then, we come but in despite.
We do not come, as minding to content you,
Our true intent is. All for your delight
We are not here. [V.i]
*The players introducing the play they are about to per-
form at the wedding*

Whereat with blade, with bloody blameful blade,
He bravely broach'd his boiling bloody breast. [V.i]
Prologue describing Pyramus's suicide

Now the hungry lion roars,
And the wolf behowls the moon;
Whilst the heavy ploughman snores,
All with weary task fordone. [V.i]
Puck describing night

If we shadows have offended,
Think but this, and all is mended,
That you have but slumb'red here
While these visions did appear.
And this weak and idle theme,
No more yielding but a dream,
Gentles, do not reprehend.
If you pardon we will mend.
And as I am an honest Puck,
If we have unearned luck
Now to scape the serpent's tongue,
We will make amends ere long;
Else the Puck a liar call.
So, good night unto you all.
Give me your hands, if we be friends,
And Robin shall restore amends. [V.i]
Puck's closing speech

Much Ado About Nothing

Written 1598-9
Time and place of action 16th-Century Messina

*Claudio loves Hero, daughter of Leonato. Don
John tries to thwart Claudio by tricking him into
believing Hero is unfaithful. Claudio denounces
Hero at their wedding ceremony; she faints and is
reported dead. Meanwhile, the mock-enemies
Beatrice and Benedick are tricked into believing
that each is in love with the other. Beatrice,
Hero's cousin, urges Benedick to avenge Hero by
killing Claudio, but then Don John's malice is
revealed; Claudio in remorse promises to marry
Leonato's niece who proves to be Hero herself. The
two couples plan a double wedding as news comes
that the runaway Don John has been captured.*

A victory is twice itself when the achiever brings
home full numbers. [I.i]
Leonato, on hearing of Don Pedro's victories at war

There is a kind of merry war between betwixt
Signior Benedick and her; they never meet but
there's a skirmish of wit between them. [I.i]
Leonato on Beatrice and Benedick's mutual antagonism

Would it not grieve a woman to be over-master'd
with a piece of valiant dust, to make an account of
her life to a clod of wayward marl? [II.i]
Beatrice telling her uncle Leonato she wants no husband

Friendship is constant in all other things
Save in the office and affairs of love;
Therefore all hearts in love use their own tongues.
Let every eye negotiate for itself,
And trust no agent: for beauty is a witch
Against whose charms faith melteth into blood. [II.i]
Claudio, on the nature of friendship and love

She speaks poniards, and every word stabs; if her
breath were as terrible as her terminations, there
were no living near her; she would infect to the
north star. I would not marry her though she were
endowed with all that Adam had left him before he
transgress'd; she would have made Hercules have
turn'd spit, yea, and have cleft his club to make the
fire too. [II.i]
Benedick talking of his dislike for Beatrice

D. Pedro: Will you have me, lady?
Beatrice: No, my lord, unless I might have another for working-days; your Grace is too costly to wear every day. [II.i]
Beatrice turning Don Pedro's offer down

She is never sad but when she sleeps, and not ever sad then; for I have heard my daughter say she hath often dreamt of unhappiness, and wak'd herself with laughing. [II.i]
Leonato talking of Beatrice's merry disposition

Sigh no more, ladies, sigh no more,
Men were deceivers ever,
One foot in sea and one on shore,
To one thing constant never.
Then sigh not so, but let them go,
And be you blithe and bonny,
Converting all your sounds of woe
Into Hey nonny nonny. [II.iii]
Song

Doth not the appetite alter? A man loves the meat in his youth that he cannot endure in his age. Shall quips, and sentences, and these paper bullets of the brain, awe a man from the career of his humour? No; the world must be peopled. When I said I would die a bachelor, I did not think I should live till I were

married. Here comes Beatrice. By this day, she's a
fair lady; I do spy some marks of love in her. [II.iii]
*Benedick, succumbing to Don Pedro, Claudio and
Leonato's trick, decides he is in love with Beatrice and
wants to marry her*

But nature never fram'd a woman's heart
Of prouder stuff than that of Beatrice.
Disdain and scorn ride sparkling in her eyes
Misprising what they look on; and her wit
Values itself so highly that to her
All matter else seems weak. She cannot love,
Nor take no shape nor project of affection,
She is so self-endeared. [III.i]
*Ursula and Hero talking of Beatrice in order to trap her
into falling in love with Benedick*

From the crown of his head to the sole of his foot,
he is all mirth; he hath twice or thrice cut Cupid's
bow-string, and the little hangman dare not shoot at
him; he hath a heart as sound as a bell, and his
tongue is the clapper; for what his heart thinks, his
tongue speaks. [III.ii]
Don Pedro describing Benedick in love

To be a well-favoured man is the gift of fortune; but
to write and read comes by nature. [III.iii]
Dogberry, to the 1st Watch

Do not live, Hero; do not ope thine eyes;
For, did I think thou wouldst not quickly die,
Thought I thy spirits were stronger than thy shames,
Myself would, on the rearward of reproaches,
Strike at thy life. Griev'd I I had but one?
Chid I for that at frugal nature's frame?
O, one too much by thee! Why had I one?
Why ever wast thou lovely in my eyes?
Why had I not, with charitable hand,
Took up a beggar's issue at my gates,
Who smirched thus and mir'd with infamy,
I might have said 'No part of it is mine;
This shame derives itself from unknown loins'?
But mine, and mine I lov'd, and mine I prais'd,
And mine that I was proud on; mine so much
That I myself was to myself not mine,
Valuing of her – why, she, O, she is fall'n
Into a pit of ink, that the wide sea
Hath drops too few to wash her clean again,
And salt too little which may season give
To her foul tainted flesh! [IV.i]
Leonato speaking of his daughter's lost reputation

I do love nothing in the world so well as you. Is not
that strange? [IV.i]
Benedick declares his love to Beatrice

O that he were here to write me down an ass! But,
masters, remember that I am an ass; though it be not
written down, yet forget not that I am an ass.
[IV.ii]
Dogberry incensed at having been (rightly) called an ass

I cannot bid you bid my daughter live –
That were impossible; but, I pray you both
Possess the people in Messina here
How innocent she died; and, if your love
Can labour aught in sad invention,
Hang her an epitaph upon her tomb
And sing it to her bones; sing it tonight. [V.i]
*Leonato tells Claudio how he can make amends for his
daughter's wrongful shame and death*

Foul words is but foul wind, and foul wind is but
foul breath, and foul breath is noisome; therefore I
will depart unkiss'd. [V.ii]
*Beatrice berates Benedick for not having fought Claudio
in a duel*

Prince, thou art sad; get thee a wife, get thee a wife.
There is no staff more reverend than one tipp'd with
horn. [V.iv]
Benedick, on the joys of being wed.

The Taming of the Shrew

Written Before 1594
Time and place of action 16th-Century Padua, and
  Petruchio's house in the country

*A nobleman plays a practical joke on a drunken
tinker. To entertain them, a play is put on in
which an autocratic father decrees that his attrac-
tive younger daughter may marry only after her
ill-tempered sister, Katherina (Kate), finds a husband. Petruchio, an adventurer, interested in
Kate's dowry, outdoes her behaviour in contrari-
ness and insists on marrying her. He then carries
the reluctant bride off, deprives her of food and
sleep and frustrates her at every turn until her will
is broken. She becomes a docile and obedient wife,
and lectures the other women on wifely duty.*

Her elder sister is so curst and shrewd
That, till the father rid his hands of her,
Master, your love must live a maid at home. [I.i]
Tranio talking to Lucentio about the shrewish Katherina

Say that she rail; why, then I'll tell her plain
She sings as sweetly as a nightingale.
Say that she frown; I'll say she looks as clear
As morning roses newly wash'd with dew.
Say she be mute, and will not speak a word;
Then I'll commend her volubility,
And say she uttereth piercing eloquence.
If she do bid me pack, I'll give her thanks,
As though she bid me stay by her a week;
If she deny to wed, I'll crave the day
When I shall ask the banns, and when be married
[II.i]
Petruchio saying how he plans to woo Katherina

You are call'd plain Kate,
And bonny Kate, and sometimes Kate the curst;
But, Kate, the prettiest Kate in Christendom,
Kate of Kate Hall, my super-dainty Kate,
For dainties are all Kates, and therefore, Kate,
Take this of me, Kate of my consolation. [II.i]
Petruchio addressing Katherina

Kiss me, Kate; we will be married a Sunday. [II.i]
Petruchio's confidence that he will wed Katherina

Thus I have politicly begun my reign,
And 'tis my hope to end successfully
My falcon now is sharp and passing empty,

And till she stoop she must not be full-gorg'd,
For then she never looks upon her lure.
Another way I have to man my haggard,
To make her come, and know her keeper's call,
That is, to watch her, as we watch these kites
That bate and beat, and will not be obedient.
She eat no meat today, nor none shall eat;
Last night she slept not, nor tonight she shall not;
As with the meat, some undeserved fault
I'll find about the making of the bed;
And here I'll fling the pillow, there the bolster,
This way the coverlet, another way the sheets;
Ay, and amid this hurly I intend
That all is done in reverend care of her –
And in conclusion, she shall watch all night;
And if she chance to nod I'll rail and brawl
And with the clamour keep her still awake.
This is a way to kill a wife with kindness,
And thus I'll curb her mad and headstrong humour.
[IV.i]
Petruchio describing how he plans to tame Katherina

A woman mov'd is like a fountain troubled –
Muddy, ill-seeming, thick, bereft of beauty,
And while it is so, none so dry or thirsty
Will deign to sip or touch one drop of it.
Thy husband is thy lord, thy life, thy keeper,
Thy head, thy sovereign; one that cares for thee,

And for thy maintenance commits his body
To painful labour both by sea and land,
To watch the night in storms, the day in cold,
Whilst thou liest warm at home, secure and safe
And craves no other tribute at thy hands
But love, fair looks, and true obedience –
Too little payment for so great a debt.
Such duty as the subject owes the prince,
Even such a woman oweth to her husband;
And when she is froward, peevish, sullen, sour,
And not obedient to his honest will,
What is she but a foul contending rebel
And graceless traitor to her loving lord?
I am asham'd that women are so simple
To offer war where they should kneel for peace;
Or seek for rule, supremacy, and sway,
When they are bound to serve, love and obey. [V.ii]
*Katherina, on the virtues of submitting to the authority
of men*

The Tempest

Written 1611-12
Time and place of action the Renaissance, a remote
  desert island

> *Prospero, Duke of Milan, more interested in magic
> than ruling, was expelled by his brother Antonio.
> Prospero and his baby daughter, Miranda, were
> cast up on a desert island where he made Caliban,
> a half human creature, and the spirit, Ariel, his
> slaves. Twelve years later Prospero engineers the
> shipwreck of Alonso, King of Naples, with his son
> Ferdinand, his brother Sebastian, counsellor
> Gonzalo and Antonio (Prospero's brother).
> Miranda and Ferdinand fall in love and their
> union is eventually blessed by Prospero. Antonio
> and Sebastian attempt to murder Alonso but are
> thwarted by Prospero. Antonio is forgiven but
> must restore the Dukedom to Prospero who
> renounces magic. They return to Italy leaving
> Caliban and Ariel free.*

The sky, it seems, would pour down stinking pitch,
But that the sea, mounting to th' welkin's cheek,
Dashes the fire out. O, I have suffered
With those that I saw suffer! A brave vessel,
Who had no doubt some noble creature in her,
Dash'd all to pieces! [I.ii]
Miranda telling her father, Prospero, of the shipwreck

You taught me language, and my profit on't
Is, I know how to curse. The red plague rid you,
For learning me your language! [I.ii]
*Caliban, on what Prospero did for him besides making
him a slave*

I might call him
A thing divine; for nothing natural
I ever saw so noble. [I.ii]
*Miranda telling Prospero about seeing Ferdinand, the
only other man she has ever seen besides her father*

No more dams I'll make for fish;
Nor fetch in firing
At requiring,
Nor scrape trenchering, nor wash dish.
'Ban 'Ban, Ca – Caliban,
Has a new master – Get a new man. [II.ii]
*Caliban sings drunkenly of his pleasure at leaving
Prospero*

I do not know
One of my sex; no woman's face remember,
Save, from my glass, mine own; nor have I seen
More that I may call men than you, good friend,
And my dear father. How features are abroad,
I am skilless of; but, by my modesty,
The jewel in my dower, I would not wish
Any companion in the world but you. [III.i]
*Miranda confessing her lack of experience of men and her
love for Ferdinand*

Miranda: I am your wife, if you will marry me;
If not, I'll die your maid. To be your fellow
You may deny me; but I'll be your servant,
Whether you will or no.
Ferdinand: My mistress, dearest;
And I thus humble ever.
Miranda: My husband, then?
Ferdinand: Ay, with a heart as willing
As bondage e'er of freedom. Here's my hand.
Miranda: And mine, with my heart in't. [III.i]
Miranda and Ferdinand declare their love

Be not afeard. The isle is full of noises,
Sounds, and sweet airs, that give delight, and hurt
not.
Sometimes a thousand twangling instruments
Will hum about mine ears; and sometime voices,
That, if I then had wak'd after long sleep,

Will make me sleep again; and then, in dreaming,
The clouds methought would open and show riches
Ready to drop upon me, that, when I wak'd,
I cried to dream again. [III.ii]
Caliban soothing Stephano's fears

Our revels now are ended. These our actors,
As I foretold you, were all spirits, and
Are melted into air, into thin air;
And, like the baseless fabric of this vision,
The cloud-capp'd towers, the gorgeous palaces,
The solemn temples, the great globe itself,
Yea, all which it inherit, shall dissolve
And, like this insubstantial pageant faded,
Leave not a rack behind. We are such stuff
As dreams are made on; and our little life
Is rounded with a sleep. [IV.i]
Prospero speaks of the vanity of human nature

This rough magic
I here abjure; and, when I have requir'd
Some heavenly music – which even now I do –
To work mine end upon their senses that
This airy charm is for, I'll break my staff,
Bury it certain fathoms in the earth,
And deeper than did ever plummet sound
I'll drown my book. [V.i]
Prospero says that he is going to give up magic

Where the bee sucks, there suck I;
In a cowslip's bell I lie;
There I couch when owls do cry.
On the bat's back I do fly
After summer merrily.
Merrily, merrily shall I live now
Under the blossom that hangs on the bough. [V.i]
Ariel's song

How many goodly creatures are there here!
How beauteous mankind is! O brave new world
That has such people in't! [V.i]
Miranda is delighted at the sight of so many humans

Retire me to my Milan, where
Every third thought shall be my grave. [V.i]
Prospero is to return to rule Milan

Twelfth Night

Written 1601
Time and place of action Renaissance Illyria

*Twins, Viola and Sebastian, are shipwrecked.
Viola believes that Sebastian is dead and disguises herself as a page called Cesario. She finds
employment with Duke Orsino with whom she
falls in love. He, however, is in love with Olivia.
Cesario acts as Orsino's messenger, taking words
of love to Olivia who falls in love with the messenger rather than the sender. When Sebastian
arrives, Olivia, mistaking him for Cesario, persuades him to marry her. Orsino is outraged
believing that he has been betrayed. When Viola
meets Sebastian she reveals her own identity.
Orsino realises that he is in love with her and
they marry. Meanwhile, Olivia's overbearing
steward, Malvolio, has been humiliated in a trick
played by her kinsman Sir Toby Belch and his
crony Sir Andrew Aguecheek.*

If music be the food of love, play on,
Give me excess of it, that, surfeiting,
The appetite may sicken and so die.
That strain again! It had a dying fall;
O, it came o'er my ear like the sweet sound
That breathes upon a bank of violets,
Stealing and giving odour! [I.i]
Duke Orsino talking of music

O, when mine eyes did see Olivia first,
Methought she purg'd the air of pestilence!
That instant was I turn'd into a hart,
And my desires, like fell and cruel hounds,
E'er since pursue me. [I.i]
The Duke describing how he fell in love with Olivia

Methinks sometimes I have no more wit than a
Christian or an ordinary man has; but I am a great
eater of beef, and I believe that does harm to my
wit. [I.iii]
Sir Andrew Aguecheek talking to Sir Toby Belch

Sir Andrew: I would I had bestowed that time in the
tongues that I have in fencing, dancing, and bear-
baiting. O, had I but followed the arts!
Sir Toby: Then hadst thou had an excellent head of
hair. [I.iii]
*Sir Andrew wishes he had spent more time learning
foreign languages*

They shall yet belie thy happy years
That say thou art a man: Diana's lip
Is not more smooth and rubious; thy small pipe
Is as the maiden's organ, shrill and sound,
And all is semblative a woman's part. [I.iv]
*The Duke commenting on the feminine appearance of
Viola, disguised as Cesario*

Not yet old enough for a man, nor young enough
for a boy; as a squash is before 'tis a peascod, or a
codling when 'tis almost an apple; 'tis with him in
standing water, between boy and man. He is very
well-favour'd, and he speaks very shrewishly; one
would think his mother's milk were scarce out of
him. [I.v]
Malvolio describing Viola, disguised as a man, to Olivia

Olivia: 'Tis in grain, sir; 'twill endure wind and
weather.
Viola: 'Tis beauty truly blent, whose red and white
Nature's own sweet and cunning hand laid on.
Lady, you are the cruell'st she alive,
If you will lead these graces to the grave,
And leave the world no copy.
Olivia: O, sir, I will not be so hard-hearted; I will
give out divers schedules of my beauty. It shall be
inventoried, and every particle and utensil labell'd
to my will: as – item, two lips indifferent red; item,

two grey eyes with lids to them; item, one neck, one
chin, and so forth. [I.v]
*Viola, disguised as Cesario, exhorting Olivia not to enter
into seclusion for seven years*

Make me a willow cabin at your gate,
And call upon my soul within the house;
Write loyal cantons of contemned love
And sing them loud even in the dead of night;
Halloo your name to the reverberate hills,
And make the babbling gossip of the air
Cry out 'Olivia!' O, you should not rest
Between the elements of air and earth
But you should pity me! [I.v]
*Viola, disguised as Cesario, talks with Olivia about not
wasting her beauty*

Duke: Thou dost speak masterly.
My life upon't, young though thou art, thine eye
Hath stay'd upon some favour that it loves;
Hath it not, boy?
Viola: A little, by your favour.
Duke: What kind of woman is't?
Viola: Of your complexion.
Duke: She is not worth thee, then. What years, i' faith?
Viola: About your years, my lord. [II.iv]
*Viola, disguised as Cesario, is revealing her love for the
Duke unbeknown to him*

Then let thy love be younger than thyself,
Or thy affection cannot hold the bent;
For women are as roses, whose fair flow'r
Being once display'd doth fall that very hour! [II.iv]
*The Duke warns Viola/Cesario against falling in love
with an older woman. A woman's beauty is soon lost*

Viola: My father had a daughter lov'd a man,
As it might be perhaps, were I a woman,
I should your lordship.
Duke: And what's her history?
Viola: A blank, my lord. She never told her love,
But let concealment, like a worm i' th' bud,
Feed on her damask cheek. She pin'd in thought;
And with a green and yellow melancholy
She sat like Patience on a monument,
Smiling at grief. Was not this love indeed?
We men may say more, swear more, but indeed
Our shows are more than will; for still we prove
Much in our vows, but little in our love. [II.iv]
*Viola, disguised as Cesario, confesses her love to the
Duke, unbeknownst to him.*

Be not afraid of greatness. Some are born great,
some achieve greatness, and some have greatness
thrust upon 'em. [II.v]
*Malvolio, reading a spurious love letter designed to make
him look a fool.*

This fellow is wise enough to play the fool;
And to do that well craves a kind of wit.
He must observe their mood on whom he jests,
The quality of persons, and the time;
And, like the haggard, check at every feather
That comes before his eye. This is a practice
As full of labour as a wise man's art;
For folly that he wisely shows is fit;
But wise men, folly-fall'n, quite taint their wit. [III.i]
Viola commenting on the skill of the jester

Olivia: Cesario, by the roses of the spring,
By maidhood, honour, truth, and every thing,
I love thee so that, maugre all thy pride,
Nor wit nor reason can my passion hide.
Do not extort thy reasons from this clause;
But rather reason thus with reason fetter:
Love sought is good, but given unsought is better.
Viola: By innocence I swear, and by my youth,
I have one heart, one bosom, and one truth,
And that no woman has; nor never none
Shall mistress be of it, save I alone. [III.i]
*Olivia has declared her love to Viola, disguised as
Cesario. Viola states that no woman will ever be mistress
of her heart*

The Two Gentlemen of Verona

Written Before 1594
Time and place of action 16th-Century Italy

*The two Veronese friends, Valentine and Proteus,
both fall in love with Silvia, daughter of the Duke
of Milan, although Proteus had been betrothed to
Julia. She follows him to Milan in disguise and
becomes his page. Because the Duke intends Silvia
to marry foolish Thurio, she and Valentine pro-
pose to elope, but Proteus betrays Valentine to the
Duke, who banishes him. Proteus rescues Silvia
from robbers and presses his unwelcome suit.
Valentine sees his treachery and defends Silvia.
The steadfast Julia's identity is revealed and
Proteus discovers whom he really loves. The Duke
pardons Valentine and the two couples marry.*

Home-keeping youth have ever homely wits. [I.i]
*Valentine to Proteus on his desire to improve himself by
travel*

Fie, fie, how wayward is this foolish love,
That like a testy babe will scratch the nurse,
And presently, all humbled, kiss the rod! [I.ii]
Julia berating herself for how she treated Lucetta

O, how this spring of love resembleth
The uncertain glory of an April day,
Which now shows all the beauty of the sun,
And by and by a cloud takes all away! [I.iii]
*Proteus talking of his love for Julia and fear that his
father might object*

Even as one heat another heat expels
Or as one nail by strength drives out another,
So the remembrance of my former love
Is by a newer object quite forgotten. [II.iv]
Proteus realising he is in love with Silvia

O heaven, were man
But constant, he were perfect! [V.iv]
Proteus chiding himself for being so fickle

The Winter's Tale

Written 1601-11
Time and place of action Legendary times, Sicilia
and Bohemia

> Leontes, King of Sicilia, becomes insanely suspi-
> cious of his wife, Hermione, and their guest,
> Polixenes, King of Bohemia. Polixenes, warned
> that he will be poisoned, escapes; Hermione is
> imprisoned and bears a daughter whom Leontes
> orders to be abandoned. Hermione is declared
> dead when Leontes disbelieves an oracular pro-
> nouncement of her innocence. The child, Perdita, is
> brought up by a shepherd in Bohemia, where even-
> tually Polixenes' son, Florizel, falls in love with
> her. Polixenes pursues them to Sicilia; the mystery
> of Perdita's birth is revealed, Leontes finds
> Hermione still alive, and all are reconciled.

We were as twinn'd lambs that did frisk i' th' sun
And bleat the one at th' other. What we chang'd
Was innocence for innocence; we knew not
The doctrine of ill-doing, nor dream'd

That any did. [I.ii]
*Polixenes, King of Bohemia, telling Hermione how he
and Leontes grew up together*

But to be paddling palms and pinching fingers,
As now they are, and making practis'd smiles
As in a looking-glass. [I.ii]
*Leontes suspects his wife and Polixenes are having an
affair*

It is an heretic that makes the fire,
Not she which burns in't. I'll not call you tyrant;
But this most cruel usage of your Queen –
Not able to produce more accusation
Than your own weak-hing'd fancy – something
savours
Of tyranny, and will ignoble make you,
Yea, scandalous to the world. [II.iii]
*Paulina berating Leontes for his irrational and cruel
treatment of the Queen*

Exit, pursued by a bear. [III.iii]
stage direction

When daffodils begin to peer,
With heigh! the doxy over the dale,
Why, then comes in the sweet o' the year,
For the red blood reigns in the winter's pale.

The white sheet bleaching on the hedge,
With heigh! the sweet birds, O, how they sing!
Doth set my pugging tooth on edge,
For a quart of ale is a dish for a king.

The lark, that tirra-lirra chants,
With heigh! with heigh! the thrush and the jay,
Are summer songs for me and my aunts,
While we lie tumbling in the hay. [IV.iii]
Song by Autolycus

For you there's rosemary and rue; these keep
Seeming and savour all the winter long. [IV.iv]
Perdita welcomes Camillo and Polixenes with flowers

Here's flow'rs for you:
Hot lavender, mints, savory, marjoram;
The marigold, that goes to bed wi' th' sun,
And with him rises weeping. [IV.iv]
Perdita to Camillo and Polixenes

O Proserpina,
For the flowers now that, frighted, thou let'st fall
From Dis's waggon! – daffodils,
That come before the swallow dares, and take
The winds of March with beauty; violets, dim
But sweeter than the lids of Juno's eyes
Or Cytherea's breath; pale primroses,

85

That die unmarried ere they can behold
Bright Phoebus in his strength – a malady
Most incident to maids; bold oxlips, and
The crown-imperial; lilies of all kinds,
The flow'r-de-luce being one. [IV.iv]
Perdita wanting to make a garland of flowers for Florizel

O, she's warm!
If this be magic, let it be an art
Lawful as eating. [V.iii]
*Hermione, whom Leontes thought was a statue, reveals
herself as alive*

THE TRAGEDIES

Antony and Cleopatra

Written 1606-7
Time and place of action c. 30 BC, Egypt and Rome

Mark Antony is bewitched by Cleopatra in Egypt, causing him to forget his duty to Rome. On his wife's death he returns to Rome and in order to bridge the rift with Octavius Cæsar he marries his sister. But Antony returns to Cleopatra and Egypt, where they crown themselves rulers of the Eastern Empire. Cæsar challenges him to a naval battle. Antony and the Egyptian army are defeated. Believing Cleopatra has betrayed him, he rages against her. She flees, sending word that she has killed herself. Antony, with nothing left to live for, also decides to kill himself. Dying, he gets word that Cleopatra is alive. He speaks to her one last time. Rather than surrender herself to Cæsar, Cleopatra kills herself with asps. Cæsar orders a grand funeral for Antony and Cleopatra.

His captain's heart,
Which in the scuffles of great fights hath burst
The buckles on his breast, reneges all temper,
And is become the bellows and the fan
To cool a gipsy's lust. [I.i]
*Philo commenting on how Antony is bewitched by his
love for Cleopatra*

Take but good note, and you shall see in him
The triple pillar of the world transform'd
Into a strumpet's fool. [I.i]
Philo describing Antony in love

Cleopatra: If it be love indeed, tell me how much.
Antony: There's beggary in the love that can be reck-
on'd.
Cloepatra: I'll set a bourn how far to be belov'd.
Antony: Then must thou needs find out new heaven,
new earth. [I.i]
Antony on how much he loves Cleopatra

These strong Egyptian fetters I must break,
Or lose myself in dotage. [I.ii]
*Antony realises that he has to break himself away from
Cleopatra if he is to be saved*

Where think'st thou he is now? Stands he or sits he?
Or does he walk? or is he on his horse?

O happy horse, to bear the weight of Antony!
Do bravely, horse; for wot'st thou whom thou
mov'st?
The demi-Atlas of this earth, the arm
And burgonet of men. He's speaking now,
Or murmuring 'Where's my serpent of old Nile?'
For so he calls me. [I.v]
Cleopatra is missing Antony who has returned to Rome
on the death of his wife

My salad days,
When I was green in judgment, cold in blood,
To say as I said then. [I.v]
Cleopatra to Charmian, speaking of her youth when she
was inexperienced

The barge she sat in, like a burnish'd throne,
Burn'd on the water. The poop was beaten gold;
Purple the sails, and so perfumed that
The winds were love-sick with them; the oars were
silver,
Which to the tune of flutes kept stroke, and made
The water which they beat to follow faster,
As amorous of their strokes. For her own person,
It beggar'd all description. She did lie
In her pavilion, cloth-of-gold, of tissue,
O'erpicturing that Venus where we see
The fancy out-work nature. On each side her

Stood pretty dimpled boys, like smiling Cupids,
With divers-colour'd fans, whose wind did seem
To glow the delicate cheeks which they did cool,
And what they undid did. [II.ii]
Enobarbus describing when Antony first saw Cleaopatra

Her gentlewomen, like the Nereides,
So many mermaids, tended her i' th' eyes,
And made their bends adornings. At the helm
A seeming mermaid steers. The silken tackle
Swell with the touches of those flower-soft hands
That yarely frame the office. From the barge
A strange invisible perfume hits the sense
Of the adjacent wharfs. The city cast
Her people out upon her; and Antony,
Enthron'd i' th' market-place, did sit alone,
Whistling to th' air; which, but for vacancy,
Had gone to gaze on Cleopatra too,
And made a gap in nature. [II.ii]
Enobarbus describing Antony's first sight of Cleopatra

Age cannot wither her, nor custom stale
Her infinite variety. Other women cloy
The appetites they feed, but she makes hungry
Where most she satisfies; for vilest things
Become themselves in her, that the holy priests
Bless her when she is riggish. [II.ii]
Enobarbus on the bewitching quality of Cleopatra's beauty

Antony
Claps on his sea-wing, and, like a doting mallard,
Leaving the fight in height, flies after her.
I never saw an action of such shame;
Experience, manhood, honour, ne'er before
Did violate so itself. [III.x]
*Scarus describing to Enobarbus the shameful retreat of
Antony, following Cleopatra in leaving the sea battle*

The witch shall die.
To the young Roman boy she hath sold me, and I fall
Under this plot. She dies for't. [IV.xii]
*Antony believes his defeat is due to Cleopatra's machina-
tions. He wants to kill her*

Go tell him I have slain myself;
Say that the last I spoke was 'Antony'
And word it, prithee, piteously. [IV.xiii]
*Cleopatra tells Charmian to tell Antony that she has
killed herself*

I will be
A bridegroom in my death, and run into 't
As to a lover's bed. [IV.xiv]
Antony about to kill himself

The miserable change now at my end
Lament nor sorrow at; but please your thoughts

In feeding them with those my former fortunes
Wherein I liv'd the greatest prince o' th' world,
The noblest; and do now not basely die,
Not cowardly put off my helmet to
My countryman – a Roman by a Roman
Valiantly vanquish'd. [IV.xv]
Antony, dying, says to look to his noble past, not his miserable death

Noblest of men, woo't die?
Hast thou no care of me? Shall I abide
In this dull world, which in thy absence is
No better than a sty? O, see, my women,
The crown o' th' earth doth melt. My lord!
O, wither'd is the garland of the war,
The soldier's pole is fall'n! Young boys and girls
Are level now with men. The odds is gone,
And there is nothing left remarkable
Beneath the visiting moon. [IV.xv]
Cleopatra laments Antony's death

His legs bestrid the ocean; his rear'd arm
Crested the world. His voice was propertied
As all the tuned spheres, and that to friends;
But when he meant to quail and shake the orb,
He was as rattling thunder. For his bounty,
There was no winter in't; an autumn 'twas
That grew the more by reaping. His delights

Were dolphin-like: they show'd his back above
The element they liv'd in. In his livery
Walk'd crowns and crownets; realms and islands
were
As plates dropp'd from his pocket. [V.ii]
Cleopatra's vision of Antony

Give me my robe, put on my crown; I have
Immortal longings in me. Now no more
The juice of Egypt's grape shall moist this lip.
Yare, yare, good Iras; quick. Methinks I hear
Antony call. I see him rouse himself
To praise my noble act. I hear him mock
The luck of Cæsar, which the gods give men
To excuse their after wrath. Husband, I come.
Now to that name my courage prove my title!
I am fire and air; my other elements
I give to baser life. [V.ii]
Cleopatra's farewell speech

She shall be buried by her Antony;
No grave upon the earth shall clip in it
A pair so famous. [V.ii]
*Cæsar finding both Cleopatra and Antony dead orders
they be buried together*

Coriolanus

Written 1607-8
Time and place of action 3rd Century BC, Rome

Coriolanus is a great Roman warrior with immense pride. His mother has played a dominant part in shaping his character. Unwilling to humble himself to the common people in order to gain consulship, as his mother urges, he is banished from Rome for his arrogance. He goes to his former enemy, Aufidius, to ally himself with the Volscians against Rome. Eventually he is persuaded by the entreaties of his mother and wife not to fight and he makes a treaty between the Volscians and Romans. But he is considered a traitor by both parties and is murdered by the Volscians.

He did it to please his mother and to be partly proud, which he is, even to the altitude of his virtue. [I.i]
The First Citizen talks of Coriolanus' attachment to his mother and his pride – the two forces that drive him

What's the matter, you dissentious rogues
That, rubbing the poor itch of your opinion,
Make yourselves scabs? [I.i]
Marcius addresses the angry citizens

Then his good report should have been my son; I
therein would have found issue. [II.i]
*Coriolanus' mother, Volumnia, tells her daughter-in-law
that if Coriolanus had been killed in battle, she would
have considered his heroic death as her son*

Where gentry, title, wisdom,
Cannot conclude but by the yea and no
Of general ignorance – it must omit
Real necessities, and give way the while
To unstable slightness. Purpose so barr'd, it
follows
Nothing is done to purpose. [III.i]
*Coriolanus says that the people should have no part in
the running of public affairs*

You common cry of curs, whose breath I hate
As reek o' th' rotten fens, whose loves I prize
As the dead carcasses of unburied men
That do corrupt my air – I banish you. [III.iii]
*Coriolanus insults the mob who have banished him from
Rome*

Despising
For you the city, thus I turn my back;
There is a world elsewhere. [III.iii]
Coriolanus' parting words to the mob

The beast
With many heads butts me away. Nay, mother,
Where is your ancient courage? You were us'd
To say extremities was the trier of spirits;
That common chances common men could bear;
That when the sea was calm all boats alike
Show'd mastership in floating; fortune's blows,
When most struck home, being gentle wounded
craves
A noble cunning. You were us'd to load me
With precepts that would make invincible
The hearts that conn'd them. [IV.i]
*Coriolanus bidding farewell to his mother and exhorting
her to be strong*

Thou hast a grim appearance, and thy face
Bears a command in't; though thy tackle's torn,
Thou show'st a noble vessel. What's thy name? [IV.v]
*Aufidius, Coriolanus's former enemy, does not recognise
him*

Let me have war, say I; it exceeds peace as far as
day does night; it's spritely, waking, audible, and

full of vent. Peace is a very apoplexy, lethargy;
mull'd, deaf, sleepy, insensible; a getter of more
bastard children than war's a destroyer of men.
[IV.v]
The First Servant is happy at the prospect of renewed war

Let the Volsces
Plough Rome and harrow Italy; I'll never
Be such a gosling to obey instinct, but stand
As if a man were author of himself
And knew no other kin. [V.iii]
*Coriolanus will ignore his mother's entreaties not to
attack Rome. He will stand alone as though without a
family.*

O, a kiss
Long as my exile, sweet as my revenge!
Now, by the jealous queen of heaven, that kiss
I carried from thee, dear, and my true lip
Hath virgin'd it e'er since. [V.iii]
Coriolanus kisses his wife

There's no man in the world
More bound to's mother, yet here he lets me prate
Like one i' th' stocks. Thou hast never in thy life
Show'd thy dear mother any courtesy,
When she, poor hen, fond of no second brood,
Has cluck'd thee to the wars, and safely home

Loaden with honour. Say my request's unjust,
And spurn me back; but if it be not so,
Thou art not honest, and the gods will plague thee,
That thou restrain'st from me the duty which
To a mother's part belongs. [V.iii]
*Coriolanus' mother continues to beseech him to make
peace with Rome*

He has betray'd your business and given up,
For certain drops of salt, your city Rome –
I say your city – to his wife and mother;
Breaking his oath and resolution like
A twist of rotten silk. [V.vi]
*Aufidius reveals that Coriolanus has made a treaty with
Rome*

Bear from hence his body,
And mourn you for him. Let him be regarded
As the most noble corse that ever herald
Did follow to his urn. [V.vi]
*Coriolanus has been slain, but he was a great warrior and
should have a fitting funeral*

Cymbeline

Written 1609-10
Time and place of action 1st Century BC, Britain and Rome

Imogen, the daughter of the King of England, Cymbeline, secretly marries Posthumus Leonatus, a poor gentleman. Her stepmother, the Queen, reveals this to Cymbeline because she wants Imogen to marry her son, Cloten. Posthumus is banished and goes to Italy, where boasting of his wife's fidelity he has a bet with Iachimo that Imogen will never betray him. Iachimo fails but manages to spend the night hidden in Imogen's bedroom where he gathers enough evidence to convince Posthumus that she has been unfaithful. He orders his wife's death, but she flees disguised as a young man. In her wanderings she finds her two brothers who had been kidnapped at birth. They help defeat the invading Roman army. Eventually Iachimo is exposed as a liar, the two sons are revealed to Cymbeline, and Posthumus is reunited with and forgiven by Imogen.

A father cruel and a step-dame false;
A foolish suitor to a wedded lady
That hath her husband banish'd. [I.vi]
Imogen reflecting on her situation

If she be furnish'd with a mind so rare,
She is alone th' Arabian bird, and I
Have lost the wager. Boldness be my friend!
Arm me, audacity. [I.vi]
Iachimo meets Imogen for the first time

Cytherea,
How bravely thou becom'st thy bed! fresh lily,
And whiter than the sheets! That I might touch!
But kiss; one kiss! Rubies unparagon'd,
How dearly they do't! 'Tis her breathing that
Perfumes the chamber thus. The flame o' th' taper
Bows toward her and would under-peep her lids
To see th' enclosed lights, now canopied
Under these windows white and azure, lac'd
With blue of heaven's own tinct. [II.ii]
*Iachimo, having hidden in the trunk in Imogen's bed-
room, sees her asleep*

On her left breast
A mole cinque-spotted, like the crimson drops
I' th' bottom of a cowslip. [II.ii]
Iachimo makes a note of Imogen's mole on her breast

For there's no motion
That tends to vice in man but I affirm
It is the woman's part. Be it lying, note it,
The woman's; flattering, hers; deceiving, hers;
Lust and rank thoughts, hers, hers; revenges, hers;
Ambitions, covetings, change of prides, disdain,
Nice longing, slanders, mutability,
All faults that man may name, nay, that hell knows,
Why, hers, in part or all; but rather all;
For even to vice
They are not constant, but are changing still
One vice but of a minute old for one
Not half so old as that. I'll write against them,
Detest them, curse them. [II.v]
Posthumus rants against womankind in general, believing that Imogen has been unfaithful.

There be many Cæsars
Ere such another Julius. Britain is
A world by itself, and we will nothing pay
For wearing our own noses. [III.i]
Cloten boldy saying they will not pay tribute to Rome

The natural bravery of your isle, which stands
As Neptune's park, ribb'd and pal'd in
With rocks unscalable and roaring waters. [III.i]
The Queen talking of Britain

O, this life
Is nobler than attending for a check,
Richer than doing nothing for a bribe,
Prouder than rustling in unpaid-for silk. [III.iii]
*Belarius in praise of the way of life they lead in the
wilderness of Wales*

What should we speak of
When we are old as you? When we shall hear
The rain and wind beat dark December, how,
In this our pinching cave, shall we discourse
The freezing hours away? We have seen nothing;
We are beastly: subtle as the fox for prey,
Like warlike as the wolf for what we eat. [III.iii]
*Arviragus complains that they only know this kind of
savage life and wonders what will they talk of when old*

You must forget to be a woman; change
Command into obedience; fear and niceness –
The handmaids of all women, or, more truly,
Woman it pretty self – into a waggish courage;
Ready in gibes, quick-answer'd, saucy, and
As quarrelous as the weasel. [III.iv]
Pisanio tells Imogen to disguise herself as a man

Society is no comfort
To one not sociable. [IV.ii]
*Imogen, disguised as a boy, asks Belarius, Guiderius and
Arviragus to leave her in the cave while they go hunting*

Hamlet

Written 1600-1601
Time and place of action 13th-Century Denmark

Hamlet, Prince of Denmark, racked with grief over his father's death, and feeling betrayed by his mother's indecently hasty marriage to his uncle Claudius, is incited to revenge by the ghost of his murdered father. Feigning madness, he determines to prove Claudius' guilt by staging a reenactment of the murder. Meanwhile, Hamlet shuns Ophelia, and mistakenly kills her father, Polonius. Claudius, suspicious of his nephew's motives, solicits the help of Rosen-crantz and Guildenstern to remove Hamlet to England where he will be killed. On the way Hamlet is captured by pirates and returns to Denmark where he finds that Ophelia has drowned herself and her brother Laertes has returned seeking revenge for his father's death. Claudius, horrified at developments, contrives a duel between Hamlet and Laertes which results in their deaths as well as those of Hamlet's mother and uncle.

Horatio says 'tis but our fantasy,
And will not let belief take hold of him
Touching this dreaded sight, twice seen of us;
Therefore I have entreated him along
With us to watch the minutes of this night,
That, if again this apparition come,
He may approve our eyes and speak to it. [I.i]
*Marcellus wants the sceptical Horatio to confirm the
ghost's appearance*

What art thou that usurp'st this time of night
Together with that fair and warlike form
In which the majesty of buried Denmark
Did sometimes march? [I.i]
Horatio asks the ghost if he is the late King of Denmark

But, soft, behold! Lo, where it comes again!
I'll cross it, though it blast me. Stay, illusion.
If thou hast any sound or use of voice,
Speak to me.
If there be any good thing to be done,
That may to thee do ease and grace to me,
Speak to me.
If thou art privy to thy country's fate,
Which happily foreknowing may avoid,
O, speak!
Or if thou hast uphoarded in thy life
Extorted treasure in the womb of earth,

For which, they say, you spirits oft walk in death,
Speak of it. Stay, and speak. [I.i]
Horatio addressing the ghost

And then it started like a guilty thing
Upon a fearful summons. [I.i]
The ghost disappearing

But look, the morn, in russet mantle clad,
Walks o'er the dew of yon high eastward hill. [I.i]
A description of sunrise

O, that this too too solid flesh would melt,
Thaw, and resolve itself into a dew!
Or that the Everlasting had not fix'd
His canon 'gainst self-slaughter! O God! God!
How weary, stale, flat, and unprofitable,
Seem to me all the uses of this world!
Fie on't! Ah, fie! 'tis an unweeded garden,
That grows to seed; things rank and gross in nature
Possess it merely. That it should come to this!
But two months dead! Nay, not so much, not two.
So excellent a king that was to this
Hyperion to a satyr; so loving to my mother,
That he might not beteem the winds of heaven
Visit her face too roughly. Heaven and earth!
Must I remember? Why, she would hang on him
As if increase of appetite had grown

By what it fed on; and yet, within a month –
Let me not think on't. Frailty, thy name is woman! –
A little month, or ere those shoes were old
With which she followed my poor father's body,
Like Niobe, all tears – why she, even she –
O God! a beast that wants discourse of reason
Would have mourn'd longer – married with my
uncle,
My father's brother; but no more like my father
Than I to Hercules. Within a month,
Ere yet the salt of most unrighteous tears
Had left the flushing in her galled eyes,
She married. O, most wicked speed, to post
With such dexterity to incestuous sheets!
It is not, nor it cannot come to good.
But break, my heart, for I must hold my tongue. [I.ii]
*Hamlet longs for death and recalls with outrage his
mother's hasty marriage to his uncle Claudius*

Thrift, thrift, Horatio! the funeral bak'd-meats
Did coldly furnish forth the marriage tables.
Would I had met my dearest foe in heaven
Or ever I had seen that day, Horatio! [I.ii]
*Hamlet describing how quickly the marriage followed on
the funeral of his father*

All is not well.
I doubt some foul play. Would the night were come!

Till then sit still, my soul. Foul deeds will rise,
Though all the earth o'erwhelm them, to men's
eyes. [I.ii]
*Hamlet believes that the appearance of his father's ghost
is evidence of some foul crime*

Do not, as some ungracious pastors do,
Show me the steep and thorny way to heaven,
Whiles, like a puff'd and reckless libertine,
Himself the primrose path of dalliance treads
And recks not his own rede. [I.iii]
*Ophelia tells her brother Laertes not to give her difficult
advice to follow and then not apply the same strictures to
himslf*

Neither a borrower nor a lender be;
For loan oft loses both itself and friend,
And borrowing dulls the edge of husbandry.
This above all – to thine own self be true,
And it must follow, as the night the day,
Thou canst not then be false to any man. [I.iii]
*Polonius gives his son, Laertes, advice before his depar-
ture for France*

Murder most foul, as in the best it is;
But this most foul, strange, and unnatural.
[I.v]
The ghost speaks to Hamlet about his murder

Thus was I, sleeping, by a brother's hand
Of life, of crown, of queen, at once dispatch'd;
Cut off even in the blossoms of my sin,
Unhous'led, disappointed, unanel'd;
No reck'ning made, but sent to my account
With all my imperfections on my head.
O, horrible! O, horrible! most horrible!
If thou hast nature in thee, bear it not. [I.v]
The ghost recounts his murder

O most pernicious woman!
O villain, villain, smiling, damned villain!
My tables – meet it is I set it down
That one may smile, and smile, and be a villain;
At least I am sure it may be so in Denmark. [I.v]
Hamlet is appalled at his mother's alliance with Claudius
the hypocritical murderer

Lord Hamlet, with his doublet all unbrac'd,
No hat upon his head, his stockings fouled,
Ungart'red and down-gyved to his ankle;
Pale as his shirt, his knees knocking each other,
And with a look so piteous in purport
As if he had been loosed out of hell
To speak of horrors – he comes before me [II.i]
Ophelia tells Polonius that Hamlet came to her looking
insane

That he's mad, 'tis true: 'tis true 'tis pity;
And pity 'tis 'tis true. A foolish figure!
But farewell it, for I will use no art. [II.ii]
*Polonius confirms to the King and Queen that Hamlet is
mad*

And he repelled, a short tale to make,
Fell into a sadness, then into a fast,
Thence to a watch, thence into a weakness,
Thence to a lightness, and, by this declension,
Into the madness wherein now he raves
And all we mourn for. [II.ii]
Polonius describes Hamlet's madness

Polonius: Do you know me, my lord?
Hamlet: Excellent well; you are a fishmonger. [II.ii]
Hamlet, pretending to be mad, toys with Polonius

Hamlet: Slanders, sir; for the satirical rogue says
here that old men have grey beards; that their faces
are wrinkled; their eyes purging thick amber and
plum-tree gum; and that they have a plentiful lack
of wit, together with most weak hams – all of
which, sir, though I most powerfully and potently
believe, yet I hold it not honestly to have it thus set
down; for you yourself, sir, shall grow old as I am,
if, like a crab, you could go backward.

Polonius: Though this be madness, yet there is method in't. [II.ii]
Polonius has asked Hamlet what is in the book that he is reading

Polonius: My lord, I will take my leave of you.
Hamlet: You cannot, sir, take from me anything that I will more willingly part withal – except my life, except my life, except my life. [II.ii]
Another example of Hamlet's madness

It goes so heavily with my disposition that this goodly frame, the earth, seems to me a sterile promontory; this most excellent canopy the air, look you, this brave o'erhanging firmament, this majestical roof fretted with golden fire – why, it appeareth no other thing to me than a foul and pestilent congregation of vapours. What a piece of work is a man! How noble in reason! how infinite in faculties! in form and moving, how express and admirable! in action, how like an angel! in apprehension, how like a god! the beauty of the world! the paragon of animals! And yet, to me, what is this quintessence of dust? Man delights not me – no, nor woman neither, though by your smiling you seem to say so. [II.ii]
Hamlet describes his depressed state to Rosencrantz and Guildenstern

I am but mad north-north-west; when the wind is
southerly I know a hawk from a handsaw. [II.ii]
Hamlet tells Guildenstern he is not really mad

I have heard
That guilty creatures, sitting at a play,
Have by the very cunning of the scene
Been struck so to the soul that presently
They have proclaim'd their malefactions;
For murder, though it have no tongue, will speak
With most miraculous organ. [II.ii]
*Hamlet believes that reconstructing the crime in a play
will expose his guilty uncle*

The play's the thing
Wherein I'll catch the conscience of the King. [II.ii]
*Hamlet plans to expose the King as the murderer of his
father*

To be, or not to be – that is the question;
Whether 'tis nobler in the mind to suffer
The slings and arrows of outrageous fortune,
Or to take arms against a sea of troubles,
And by opposing end them? To die, to sleep –
No more; and by a sleep to say we end
The heart-ache and the thousand natural shocks
That flesh is heir to. 'Tis a consummation
Devoutly to be wish'd. To die, to sleep;

To sleep, perchance to dream. Ay, there's the rub;
For in that sleep of death what dreams may come,
When we have shuffled off this mortal coil,
Must give us pause. There's the respect
That makes calamity of so long life;
For who would bear the whips and scorns of time,
Th' oppressor's wrong, the proud man's contumely,
The pangs of despis'd love, the law's delay,
The insolence of office, and the spurns
That patient merit of th' unworthy takes,
When he himself might his quietus make
With a bare bodkin? Who would these fardels bear,
To grunt and sweat under a weary life,
But that the dread of something after death –
The undiscover'd country, from whose bourn
No traveller returns – puzzles the will,
And makes us rather bear those ills we have
Than fly to others that we know not of?
Thus conscience does make cowards of us all;
And thus the native hue of resolution
Is sicklied o'er with the pale cast of thought,
And enterprises of great pitch and moment,
With this regard, their currents turn awry
And lose the name of action. [III.i]
Hamlet soliloquising on the value of life

Get thee to a nunnery. Why wouldst thou be a
breeder of sinners? I am myself indifferent honest,

but yet I could accuse me of such things that it were
better my mother had not borne me: I am very
proud, revengeful, ambitious; with more offences at
my beck than I have thoughts to put them in, imagination to give them shape, or time to act them in.
What should such fellows as I do crawling between
earth and heaven? We are arrant knaves, all; believe
none of us. [III.i]
*Hamlet viciously rejects Ophelia convincing her of his
madness*

O, what a noble mind is here o'erthrown!
The courtier's, soldier's, scholar's, eye, tongue, sword;
Th' expectancy and rose of the fair state,
The glass of fashion and the mould of form,
Th' observ'd of all observers – quite, quite down!
And I, of ladies most deject and wretched,
That suck'd the honey of his music vows,
Now see that noble and most sovereign reason,
Like sweet bells jangled, out of time and harsh;
That unmatch'd form and feature of blown youth
Blasted with ecstasy. O, woe is me
T' have seen what I have seen, see what I see! [III.i]
Ophelia is distraught at Hamlet's behaviour

Be not too tame neither, but let your own discretion
be your tutor. Suit the action to the word, the word
to the action; with this special observance, that you

o'erstep not the modesty of nature; for anything so
o'erdone is from the purpose of playing, whose end,
both at the first and now, was and is to hold, as
'twere, the mirror up to nature; to show virtue her
own feature, scorn her own image, and the very age
and body of the time his form and pressure. Now,
this overdone or come tardy off, though it makes
the unskilful laugh, cannot but make the judicious
grieve; the censure of which one must, in your
allowance, o'erweigh a whole theatre of others. O,
there be players that I have seen play – and heard
others praise, and that highly – not to speak it pro-
fanely, that, neither having th' accent of Christians,
nor the gait of Christian, pagan, nor man, have so
strutted and bellowed that I have thought some of
Nature's journeymen had made men, and not made
them well, they imitated humanity so abominably.
[III.ii]
Hamlet lecturing the Players on acting

The lady doth protest too much, methinks. [III.ii]
The Queen's comment on the female character in the play

Hamlet: No, no; they do but jest, poison in jest; no
offence i' th' world.
King: What do you call the play?
Hamlet: 'The Mouse-trap.' [III.ii]
*The name of the play with which Hamlet hopes to trap
the King*

'Tis now the very witching time of night,
When churchyards yawn, and hell itself breathes out
Contagion to this world. Now could I drink hot blood,
And do such bitter business as the day
Would quake to look on. [III.ii]
Hamlet plotting his revenge

Let me be cruel, not unnatural:
I will speak daggers to her, but use none. [III.ii]
Hamlet of his mother

O, my offence is rank, it smells to heaven;
It hath the primal eldest curse upon't–
A brother's murder! [III.iii]
The King soliloquises about his crime

My words fly up, my thoughts remain below.
Words without thoughts never to heaven go. [III.iii]
The King, although he wants forgiveness, cannot repent his crime

A bloody deed! – almost as bad, good mother,
As kill a king and marry with his brother. [III.iv]
Hamlet to his mother after he has killed Polonius

Thou wretched, rash, intruding fool, farewell!
I took thee for thy better. [III.iv]
Hamlet addressing the body of Polonius whom he'd mistaken for his uncle

Look here upon this picture and on this,
The counterfeit presentment of two brothers.
See what a grace was seated on this brow;
Hyperion's curls; the front of Jove himself;
An eye like Mars, to threaten and command;
A station like the herald Mercury
New lighted on a heaven-kissing hill –
A combination and a form indeed
Where every god did seem to set his seal,
To give the world assurance of a man.
This was your husband. Look you now what follows:
Here is your husband, like a mildew'd ear
Blasting his wholesome brother. Have you eyes?
Could you on this fair mountain leave to feed,
And batten on this moor? Ha! Have you eyes?
You cannot call it love; for at your age
The heyday in the blood is tame, it's humble,
And waits upon the judgement; and what judge-
ment
Would step from this to this? [III.iv]
*Hamlet making his mother compare the portraits of her
former husband and her new husband*

Nay, but to live
In the rank sweat of an enseamed bed,
Stew'd in corruption, honeying and making love
Over the nasty sty! [III.iv]
Hamlet to his mother

I must be cruel, only to be kind. [III.iv]
Hamlet is justifying his behaviour

Rightly to be great
Is not to stir without great argument,
But greatly to find quarrel in a straw,
When honour's at the stake. How stand I, then,
That have a father kill'd, a mother stain'd,
Excitements of my reason and my blood,
And let all sleep, while to my shame I see
The imminent death of twenty thousand men
That, for a fantasy and trick of fame,
Go to their graves like beds, fight for a plot
Whereon the numbers cannot try the cause,
Which is not tomb enough and continent
To hide the slain? O, from this time forth,
My thoughts be bloody, or be nothing worth! [IV.iv]
*Hamlet is shamed that he is unable to avenge his father's
death comparing his impotence to the twenty thousand
men who would willingly die for some inconsequential
territory*

He is dead and gone, lady,
He is dead and gone;
At his head a grass-green turf,
At his heels a stone. [IV.v]
*Ophelia has gone mad and is singing a song about a
death*

Lord, we know what we are, but know not what we
may be. [IV.v]
Ophelia rambling

When sorrows come, they come not single spies,
But in battalions. [IV.v]
The King talking of how one disaster has caused another

Let him go, Gertrude; do not fear our person:
There's such divinity doth hedge a king
That treason can but peep to what it would,
Acts little of his will. [IV.v]
The King speaks of the divinity of kings

To hell, allegiance! Vows, to the blackest devil!
Conscience and grace, to the profoundest pit!
I dare damnation. [IV.v]
Laertes seeks revenge for his father's murder

It warms the very sickness in my heart
That I shall live and tell him to his teeth
'Thus didest thou'. [IV.vii]
*Laertes plans to kill Hamlet in revenge for his father's
killing*

There is a willow grows aslant the brook
That shows his hoar leaves in the glassy stream;

There with fantastic garlands did she make,
Of crowflowers, nettles, daisies, and long purples
That liberal shepherds give a grosser name,
But our cold maids do dead men's fingers call them.
There, on the pendent boughs her coronet weeds
Clamb'ring to hang, an envious sliver broke;
When down her weedy trophies and herself
Fell in the weeping brook. Her clothes spread wide
And, mermaid-like, awhile they bore her up;
Which time she chanted snatches of old lauds,
As one incapable of her own distress. [IV.vii]
The Queen describing Ophelia's death by drowning

Alas, poor Yorick! I knew him, Horatio: a fellow of
infinite jest, of most excellent fancy; he hath borne
me on his back a thousand times. And now how
abhorred in my imagination it is! My gorge rises at
it. Here hung those lips that I have kiss'd I know
not how oft. Where be your gibes now, your gam-
bols, your songs, your flashes of merriment that
were wont to set the table on a roar? Not one now
to mock your own grinning – quite chap-fall'n?
Now get you to my lady's chamber, and tell her, let
her paint an inch thick, to this favour she must
come; make her laugh at that. [V.1]
*Hamlet reflects on the skull of a former court jester whom
he knew and on the inevitability of death*

Sweets to the sweet; farewell!
I hop'd thou shouldst have been my Hamlet's wife;
I thought thy bride-bed to have deck'd, sweet maid,
And not have strew'd thy grave. [V.i]
The Queen scattering flowers on Ophelia's grave

I lov'd Ophelia: forty thousand brothers
Could not, with all their quantity of love,
Make up my sum. [V.i]
Hamlet declares how much he loved Ophelia

There's a divinity that shapes our ends,
Rough-hew them how we will. [V.ii]
Hamlet to Horatio

If thou didst ever hold me in thy heart,
Absent thee from felicity awhile,
And in this harsh world draw thy breath in pain,
To tell my story. [V.ii]
*Hamlet asks Horatio not to drink the poison but to
remain alive and tell his story*

Let four captains
Bear Hamlet like a soldier to the stage;
For he was likely, had he been put on,
To have prov'd most royal. [V.ii]
Fortinbras arranges for Hamlet to be borne away

Julius Cæsar

Written 1599
Time and place of action 44 BC, Rome

Jealous and suspicious of Julius Cæsar's growing powerhold, Cassius and other leading Roman citizens conspire to assassinate him. They persuade Brutus to join their ranks by arguing that it is for the good of the republic. Cæsar is murdered in the Senate-House. Antony, Cæsar's friend, is asked to give the funeral speech and he incites the people to fury against the conspirators. Cæsar's nephew, Octavius, together with Antony and Lepidus become the new triumvirs ruling the republic. They oppose the forces of Cassius and Brutus who are defeated and subsequently commit suicide.

You blocks, you stones, you worse than senseless things!
O you hard hearts, you cruel men of Rome,
Knew you not Pompey? [I.i]
The tribunes are unhappy at Cæsar's popular welcome

Cæsar: Who is it in the press that calls on me?
I hear a tongue, shriller than all the music,
Cry 'Cæsar!' Speak. Cæsar is turn'd to hear.
Soothsayer: Beware the ides of March. [I.ii]
Cæsar is warned

Why, man, he doth bestride the narrow world
Like a Colossus, and we petty men
Walk under his huge legs, and peep about
To find ourselves dishonourable graves.
Men at some time are masters of their fates:
The fault, dear Brutus, is not in our stars,
But in ourselves, that we are underlings.
'Brutus' and 'Cæsar'. What should be in that
'Cæsar'?
Why should that name be sounded more than
yours? [I.ii]
*Cassius tells Brutus that there is no reason for Cæsar to
be so revered*

Now, in the names of all the gods at once,
Upon what meat doth this our Cæsar feed,
That he is grown so great? [I.ii]
Cassius resents Cæsar's position

Let me have men about me that are fat;
Sleek-headed men, and such as sleep o' nights.
Yond Cassius has a lean and hungry look;

He thinks too much. Such men are dangerous. [I.ii]
Cæsar is rightly suspicious of Cassius

Would he were fatter! But I fear him not.
Yet if my name were liable to fear,
I do not know the man I should avoid
So soon as that spare Cassius. He reads much,
He is a great observer, and he looks
Quite through the deeds of men. He loves no plays,
As thou dost, Antony; he hears no music.
Seldom he smiles, and smiles in such a sort
As if he mock'd himself, and scorn'd his spirit
That could be mov'd to smile at anything.
Such men as he be never at heart's ease
Whiles they behold a greater than themselves,
And therefore are they very dangerous.
I rather tell thee what is to be fear'd
Than what I fear; for always I am Cæsar. [I.ii]
Cæsar is supremely self-confident

But men may construe things after their own fashion,
Clean from the purpose of the things themselves. [I.iii]
*Cicero to Casca stating that men may interpret omens in
their own way, which is often a long way from the truth*

'Tis a common proof
That lowliness is young ambition's ladder,
Whereto the climber-upward turns his face;

But when he once attains the upmost round,
He then unto the ladder turns his back,
Looks in the clouds, scorning the base degrees
By which he did ascend. [II.i]
Brutus meditates on the nature of ambition clothed in
misleading humility

Between the acting of a dreadful thing
And the first motion, all the interim is
Like a phantasma or a hideous dream.
The Genius and the mortal instruments
Are then in council; and the state of man,
Like to a little kingdom, suffers then
The nature of an insurrection. [II.i]
Brutus does not know whether to be party to the assassi-
nation of Cæsar

Portia: Dwell I but in the suburbs
Of your good pleasure? If it be no more,
Portia is Brutus' harlot, not his wife.
Brutus: You are my true and honourable wife,
As dear to me as are the ruddy drops
That visit my sad heart. [II.i]
Portia wants Brutus to confide in her and tries to per-
suade him with the argument that if he doesn't confide in
her, she might as well be a whore

Danger knows full well
That Cæsar is more dangerous than he:
We are two lions litter'd in one day,
And I the elder and more terrible;
And Cæsar shall go forth. [II.ii]
Cæsar claims to his wife that he and danger are twins,
but he is the more powerful

Cæsar: The ides of March are come.
Soothsayer: Ay, Cæsar, but not gone. [III.i]
The Soothsayer warns Cæsar to be wary, the day isn't over

If I could pray to move, prayers would move me;
But I am constant as the northern star,
Of whose true-fix'd and resting quality
There is no fellow in the firmament.
The skies are painted with unnumb'red sparks,
They are all fire, and every one doth shine;
But there's but one in all doth hold his place.
So in the world: 'tis furnish'd well with men,
And men are flesh and blood, and apprehensive;
Yet in the number I do know but one
That unassailable holds on his rank,
Unshak'd of motion; and that I am he,
Let me a little show it, even in this –
That I was constant Cimber should be banish'd,
And constant do remain to keep him so. [III.i]
Cæsar addressing the Senate

Et tu, Brute? – Then fall, Cæsar! [III.i]
Cæsar to Brutus on being stabbed

Cassius: How many ages hence
Shall this our lofty scene be acted over
In states unborn and accents yet unknown!
Brutus: How many times shall Cæsar bleed in sport.
[III.i]
*Cassius forsees the time when Cæsar's death will be re-
enacted on the stage*

Had I as many eyes as thou hast wounds,
Weeping as fast as they stream forth thy blood,
It would become me better than to close
In terms of friendship with thine enemies. [III.i]
*Antony would rather shed tears than form an alliance
with Cæsar's murderers*

O, pardon me, thou bleeding piece of earth,
That I am meek and gentle with these butchers!
Thou art the ruins of the noblest man
That ever lived in the tide of times.
Woe to the hand that shed this costly blood! [III.i]
*Antony soliloquises about Cæsar's death and how he
plans to avenge it*

Cæsar's spirit, ranging for revenge,
With Atè by his side come hot from hell,

Shall in these confines with a monarch's voice
Cry 'Havoc!' and let slip the dogs of war,
That this foul deed shall smell above the earth
With carrion men, groaning for burial. [III.i]
Antony plans to launch a civil war

Not that I lov'd Cæsar less, but that I lov'd Rome
more. [III.ii]
*Brutus addresses Plebeians trying to justify why Cæsar
was killed*

As he was valiant, I honour him; but – as he was
ambitious, I slew him. [III.ii]
*Brutus claims that Cæsar's ambition was the reason for
his death*

Friends, Romans, countrymen, lend me your ears;
I come to bury Cæsar, not to praise him.
The evil that men do lives after them;
The good is oft interred with their bones;
So let it be with Cæsar. The noble Brutus
Hath told you Cæsar was ambitious.
If it were so, it was a grievous fault;
And grievously hath Cæsar answer'd it.
Here, under leave of Brutus and the rest –
For Brutus is an honourable man;
So are they all, all honourable men –
Come I to speak in Cæsar's funeral. [III.ii]
Antony gives the funeral oration for Cæsar

He was my friend, faithful and just to me;
But Brutus says he was ambitious,
And Brutus is an honourable man. [III.ii]
*Antony ironically reminds the crowd that Brutus
claimed Cæsar was ambitious*

On the Lupercal
I thrice presented him a kingly crown,
Which he did thrice refuse. Was this ambition? [III.ii]
*Antony gives an example of how Cæsar was not ambi-
tious contradicting Brutus' claim*

This was the most unkindest cut of all;
For when the noble Cæsar saw him stab,
Ingratitude, more strong than traitors' arms,
Quite vanquish'd him. Then burst his mighty heart;
And in his mantle muffling up his face,
Even at the base of Pompey's statua,
Which all the while ran blood, great Cæsar fell.
O, what a fall was there, my countrymen!
Then I, and you, and all of us fell down,
Whilst bloody treason flourish'd over us.
O, now you weep, and I perceive you feel
The dint of pity. These are gracious drops. [III.ii]
*Antony tells the Plebeians how Cæsar was betrayed by
Brutus*

For I have neither wit, nor words, nor worth,
Action, nor utterance, nor the power of speech,

To stir men's blood; I only speak right on.
I tell you that which you yourselves do know. [III.ii]
Antony claiming not to be a good orator

But were I Brutus,
And Brutus Antony, there were an Antony
Would ruffle up your spirits, and put a tongue
In every wound of Cæsar, that should move
The stones of Rome to rise and mutiny. [III.ii]
Antony wants to provoke civil war

Did not Julius bleed for justice' sake?
What villain touch'd his body, that did stab,
And not for justice? What shall one of us,
That struck the foremost man of all this world
But for supporting robbers, shall we now
Contaminate our fingers with base bribes,
And sell the mighty space of our large honours
For so much trash as may be grasped thus?
I had rather be a dog and bay the moon
Than such a Roman. [IV.iii]
*Brutus justifies his part in the murder stating he did it
for justice. Therefore there is no way he would accept
bribes*

A friend should bear his friend's infirmities,
But Brutus makes mine greater than they are. [IV.iii]
Cassius to Brutus who has accused him of bribery

Cassius is aweary of the world:
Hated by one he loves; brav'd by his brother;
Check'd like a bondman; all his faults observ'd,
Set in a notebook, learn'd, and conn'd by rote,
To cast into my teeth. [IV.iii]
Cassius would be happy to be slain by his enemies, since his friend Brutus has criticized him

The enemy increaseth every day:
We, at the height, are ready to decline.
There is a tide in the affairs of men
Which, taken at the flood, leads on to fortune;
Omitted, all the voyage of their life
Is bound in shallows and in miseries.
On such a full sea are we now afloat,
And we must take the current when it serves,
Or lose our ventures. [IV.iii]
Brutus says they must act quickly i.e. march on the enemy, if they are to succeed

O that a man might know
The end of this day's business ere it come!
But it sufficeth that the day will end,
And then the end is known. [V.i]
Brutus, marching into battle, would like to know the outcome

This day I breathed first. Time is come round,
And where I did begin there shall I end;
My life is run his compass. [V.iii]
Cassius is convinced his own death is near: he will come
full circle by dying on his birthday

O Julius Cæsar, thou art mighty yet!
Thy spirit walks abroad and turns our swords
In our own proper entrails. [V.iii]
Brutus realises that Cæsar's spirit is not yet dead

Thou art a fellow of a good respect;
Thy life hath had some smatch of honour in it.
Hold then my sword, and turn away thy face,
While I do run upon it. [V.v]
Brutus to Strato just before he commits suicide

This was the noblest Roman of them all.
All the conspirators save only he
Did that they did in envy of great Cæsar;
He only in a general honest thought
And common good to all made one of them.
His life was gentle; and the elements
So mix'd in him that Nature might stand up
And say to all the world 'This was a man!' [V v]
Antony's tribute to Brutus

King Lear

Written 1605
Time and place of action Primitive Britain

King Lear decides to divide his kingdom between his three daughters, Goneril, Regan and Cordelia, depending on how much they love him. Goneril and Regan heap him with flattery but Cordelia, his favourite, refuses to exaggerate her love. Enraged, he disinherits her leaving his wealth to the other two. The King of France marries the dowryless Cordelia. When Lear visits Goneril she begrudges looking after her father and he leaves furious. Regan treats him just as badly, and the old man rushes out into a storm. He gets to Dover where Cordelia has landed with the French to help her father. Goneril is poisoned by Regan because of a rival love affair with Edmund, Gloucester's illegitimate son, who has turned his father against his legitimate brother Edgar. Regan then kills herself. The English defeat the French and Cordelia and Lear are imprisoned. Cordelia is hanged and Lear dies from grief for the daughter who really did love him.

Cordelia: You have begot me, bred me, lov' me; I
Return those duties back as are right fit,
Obey you, love you, and most honour you.
Why have my sisters husbands, if they say
They love you all? Haply, when I shall wed,
That lord whose hand must take my plight shall carry
Half my love with him, half my care and duty.
Sure I shall never marry like my sisters,
To love my father all.
Lear: But goes thy heart with this?
Cordelia: Ay, my good lord.
Lear: So young and so untender?
Cordelia: So young, my lord, and true.
Lear: Let it be so! Thy truth, then, be thy dower!
For, by the sacred radiance of the sun,
The mysteries of Hecat and the night;
By all the operation of the orbs
From whom we do exist and cease to be;
Here I disclaim all my paternal care,
Propinquity and property of blood,
And as a stranger to my heart and me
Hold thee from this for ever. [I.i]
*Cordelia refuses to flatter her father as her sisters have
done. Enraged, he casts her off*

Come not between the dragon and his wrath. [I.i]
*King Lear warns Kent not to intervene on Cordelia's
behalf*

Love's not love
When it is mingled with regards that stand
Aloof from th' entire point. [I.i]
*The King of France is asking Burgundy if he still wants
to marry Cordelia*

Fairest Cordelia, that art most rich, being poor;
Most choice, forsaken; and most lov'd, despis'd!
Thee and thy virtues here I seize upon,
Be it lawful I take up what's cast away. [I.i]
*France wants to marry Cordelia despite her being disin-
herited and banished*

Why bastard? Wherefore base?
When my dimensions are as well compact,
My mind as generous, and my shape as true,
As honest madam's issue? Why brand they us
With base? with baseness? bastardy? base, base?
Who, in the lusty stealth of nature, take
More composition and fierce quality
Than doth, within a dull, stale, tired bed,
Go to th' creating a whole tribe of fops
Got 'tween asleep and wake? [I.ii]
Edmund bewails attitudes towards illegitimacy

This is the excellent foppery of the world, that,
when we are sick in fortune, often the surfeits of our
own behaviour, we make guilty of our disasters the

sun, the moon, and stars; as if we were villains on
necessity; fools by heavenly compulsion; knaves,
thieves, and treachers, by spherical predominance;
drunkards, liars, and adulterers, by an enforc'd
obedience of planetary influence; and all that we are
evil in, by a divine thrusting on – an admirable eva-
sion of whoremaster man, to lay his goatish disposition on the charge of a star! My father compounded
with my mother under the Dragon's tail, and my
nativity was under Ursa Major, so that it follows I
am rough and lecherous. Fut, I should have been
that I am, had the maidenliest star in the firmament
twinkled on my bastardizing. [I.ii]
*Edmund on how men blame things on forces outside their
control*

Have more than thou showest,
Speak less than thou knowest,
Lend less than thou owest,
Ride more than thou goest,
Learn more than thou trowest;
Set less than thou throwest;
Leave thy drink and thy whore,
And keep in-a-door,
And thou shalt have more
Than two tens to a score. [I.iv]
The Fool advises King Lear

Lear: Dost thou call me fool, boy?
Fool: All thy other titles thou hast given away; that thou wast born with. [I.iv]
The Fool makes fun of King Lear for having given away his land

Ingratitude, thou marble-hearted fiend,
More hideous, when thou show'st thee in a child
Than the sea-monster! [I.iv]
King Lear is outraged by Goneril's behaviour to him

How sharper than a serpent's tooth it is
To have a thankless child. [I.iv]
King Lear at last realises that Goneril does not love him

O, sir, you are old;
Nature in you stands on the very verge
Of her confine. You should be rul'd and led
By some discretion that discerns your state
Better than you yourself. [II.iv]
Regan tells King Lear he is old and should have submitted to Goneril

I will not trouble thee, my child; farewell.
We'll no more meet, no more see one another.
But yet thou art my flesh, my blood, my daughter;
Or rather a disease that's in my flesh,
Which I must needs call mine. [II.iv]
King Lear to Goneril

O, reason not the need! Our basest beggars
Are in the poorest thing superfluous.
Allow not nature more than nature needs,
Man's life is cheap as beast's. Thou art a lady;
If only to go warm were gorgeous,
Why, nature needs not what thou gorgeous wear'st,
Which scarcely keeps thee warm. But for true need –
You heavens, give me that patience, patience I need.
You see me here, you gods, a poor old man,
As full of grief as age; wretched in both. [II.iv]
King Lear to his daughters on how few our real needs are

Touch me with noble anger,
And let not women's weapons, water-drops,
Stain my man's cheeks! No, you unnatural hags,
I will have such revenges on you both
That all the world shall – I will do such things –
What they are yet I know not; but they shall be
The terrors of the earth. You think I'll weep.
No, I'll not weep.
I have full cause of weeping; but this heart
Shall break into a hundred thousand flaws
Or ere I'll weep. O fool, I shall go mad! [II.iv]
*King Lear, outraged at his daughters' treatment of him,
wants revenge*

Rumble thy bellyful. Spit, fire; spout, rain.
Nor rain, wind, thunder, fire, are my daughters.

I tax not you, you elements, with unkindness;
I never gave you kingdom, call'd you children;
You owe me no subscription. Then let fall
Your horrible pleasure. Here I stand, your slave,
A poor, infirm, weak and despis'd old man;
But yet I call you servile ministers
That will with two pernicious daughters join
Your high-engender'd battles 'gainst a head
So old and white as this. [III.ii]
*King Lear invokes the elements against his ungrateful
daughters*

The art of our necessities is strange
That can make vile things precious. [III.ii]
King Lear is happy to take shelter in a hovel

Poor naked wretches, wheresoe'er you are,
That bide the pelting of this pitiless storm,
How shall your houseless heads and unfed sides,
Your loop'd and window'd raggedness, defend you
From seasons such as these? O, I have ta'en
Too little care of this! Take physic, pomp;
Expose thyself to feel what wretches feel. [III.iv]
*King Lear regrets the fact that when he ruled he had no
thought of the poor and needy*

Child Rowland to the dark tower came,
His word was still 'Fie, foh, and fum,

I smell the blood of a British man'. [III.iv]
Edgar pretending to be a roaming lunatic

He's mad that trusts in the tameness of a wolf, a
horse's health, a boy's love, or a whore's oath. [III.vi]
The Fool to King Lear

Cornwall: Out vile jelly!
Where is thy lustre now?
Gloucester: All dark and comfortless! [III.vii]
Cornwall puts out Gloucester's eyes

Yet better thus and known to be contemn'd,
Than still contemn'd and flatter'd. To be worst,
The lowest and most dejected thing of fortune,
Stands still in esperance, lives not in fear.
The lamentable change is from the best;
The worst returns to laughter. [IV.i]
*Edgar reflecting that even the most wretched state has
things to be said in its favour*

I have no way, and therefore want no eyes;
I stumbled when I saw. [IV.i]
Gloucester, blinded, being led by an old man

As flies to wanton boys are we to th' gods –
They kill us for their sport. [IV.i]
Gloucester lamenting how fate is treating him

Wisdom and goodness to the vile seem vile;
Filths savour but themselves. What have you done?
Tigers, not daughters, what have you perform'd?
A father, and a gracious aged man,
Whose reverence even the head-lugg'd bear would
lick,
Most barbarous, most degenerate, have you
madded. [IV.ii]
*Albany berating his wife, Goneril, for her evil behaviour
towards her father*

And now and then an ample tear trill'd down
Her delicate cheek. It seem'd she was a queen
Over her passion, who, most rebel-like,
Sought to be king o'er her. [IV.iii]
Cordelia's tears on reading a letter about her father's state

How fearful
And dizzy 'tis to cast one's eyes so low!
The crows and choughs that wing the midway air
Show scarce so gross as beetles. Half-way down
Hangs one that gathers samphire – dreadful trade!
Methinks he seems no bigger than his head.
The fishermen that walk upon the beach
Appear like mice; and yond tall anchoring bark
Diminish'd to her cock; her cock, a buoy
Almost too small for sight. The murmuring surge
That on th' unnumb'red idle pebble chafes

Cannot be heard so high. [IV.vi]
Edgar describes the cliffs of Dover to Gloucester, pretending that they have reached the edge

Lear: The fitchew nor the soiled horse goes to't
With a more riotous appetite.
Down from the waist they are centaurs,
Though women all above;
But to the girdle do the gods inherit,
Beneath is all the fiends';
There's hell, there's darkness, there is the sul-
phurous pit –
Burning, scalding, strench, consumption.
Fie, fie, fie! pah, pah! GIve me an ounce of civet,
good apothecary, to sweeten my imagination.
There's money for thee.
Gloucester: O, let me kiss that hand!
Lear: Let me wipe it first; it smells of mortality.
Gloucester: O ruin'd piece of nature! This great world
Shall so wear out to nought. [IV.vi]
Gloucester has recognized the voice of King Lear who is raving about the horrors of sexuality

Through tatter'd clothes small vices do appear;
Robed and furr'd gowns hide all. Plate sin with gold,
And the strong lance of justice hurtless breaks;
Arm it in rags, a pigmy's straw doth pierce it. [IV.vi]
King Lear on there being one law for the rich and another for the poor

When we are born, we cry that we are come
To this great stage of fools. [IV.vi]
King Lear to Gloucester

Thou art a soul in bliss; but I am bound
Upon a wheel of fire, that mine own tears
Do scald like molten lead. [IV.vii]
*King Lear thinks he is dead, and when he sees Cordelia he
thinks she is a spirit*

Men must endure
Their going hence, even as their coming hither:
Ripeness is all. [V.ii]
Edgar on the necessity of succumbing to fate

Come, let's away to prison.
We two alone will sing like birds i' th' cage;
When thou dost ask me blessing, I'll kneel down
And ask of thee forgiveness; so we'll live,
And pray, and sing, and tell old tales, and laugh
At gilded butterflies, and hear poor rogues
Talk of court news; and we'll talk with them too –
Who loses and who wins; who's in, who's out –
And take upon's the mystery of things
As if we were God's spies; and we'll wear out
In a wall'd prison packs and sects of great ones
That ebb and flow by th' moon. [V.iii]
King Lear on going to prison with Cordelia

The wheel is come full circle. [V.iii]
*Edmund on being brought down by his half-brother
Edgar*

Howl, howl, howl, howl! O, you are men of stones!
Had I your tongues and eyes, I'd use them so
That heaven's vault should crack. She's gone for
ever. [V.iii]
King Lear carrying the dead Cordelia

Her voice was ever soft,
Gentle, and low – an excellent thing in woman.
[V.iii]
King Lear describing Cordelia

And my poor fool is hang'd! No, no, no life?
Why should a dog, a horse, a rat have life,
And thou no breath at all? Thou'lt come no more,
Never, never, never, never, never.
Pray you undo this button. [V.iii]
King Lear on the injustice of Cordelia's death

The weight of this sad time we must obey;
Speak what we feel, not what we ought to say.
The oldest hath borne most; we that are young
Shall never see so much nor live so long. [V.iii]
*Edgar as the play finishes and he is surrounded by the
dead. He believes such sorrows will not be seen again*

Macbeth

Written 1606
Time and place of action 11th-Century Scotland

Macbeth and Banquo encounter three witches who prophesy that Macbeth will become first Thane of Cawdor then king, and that Banquo will beget kings. News that Macbeth has been made Thane of Cawdor substantiates the prophecies. Lady Macbeth, ruthlessly ambitious, determines to ensure that the second prophecy will come true. Duncan, King of Scotland, is visiting and she plots his death persuading Macbeth to carry it out. Macbeth is made king and has Banquo murdered. Haunted by Banquo's ghost, Macbeth returns to the witches. They say 'none of woman born shall harm him' and to only worry when Birnam wood moves to Dunsinane. Macbeth becomes a murderous tyrant. Lady Macbeth, tormented by her memories, kills herself. Macbeth, while realising the futility of what he has achieved, thinks he is safe. However, the woods (men camouflaged with branches) do move and the man 'none of woman born' is Macduff (born by

Cæsarian section), whose family have been killed on Macbeth's orders. He kills Macbeth and Malcolm becomes king.

First Witch: When shall we three meet again?
In thunder, lightning, or in rain?
Second Witch: When the hurlyburly's done,
When the battle's lost and won.
Third Witch: That will be ere the set of sun.
First Witch: Where the place?
Second Witch: Upon the heath.
Third Witch: There to meet with Macbeth.
First Witch: I come, Graymalkin.
Second Witch: Paddock calls.
Third Witch: Anon!
All: Fair is foul, and foul is fair:
Hover through the fog and filthy air. [I.i]
The three witches

Brave Macbeth – well he deserves that name –
Disdaining Fortune, with his brandish'd steel
Which smok'd with bloody execution,
Like valour's minion, carv'd out his passage
Till he fac'd the slave;
Which ne'er shook hands, nor bade farewell to him,
Till he unseam'd him from the nave to th' chaps,
And fix'd his head upon our battlements. [I.ii]
Sergeant describing Macbeth's bravery in defeating the rebel Macdonwald

So foul and fair a day I have not seen. [I.iii]
Macbeth on winning a victory in bad weather

What are these,
So withered, and so wild in their attire,
That look not like th' inhabitants o' th' earth,
And yet are on 't? Live you, or are you aught
That man may question? You seem to understand
me,
By each at once her choppy finger laying
Upon her skinny lips. You should be women,
And yet your beards forbid me to interpret
That you are so. [I.iii]
Banquo and Macbeth come across the three witches

If you can look into the seeds of time
And say which grain will grow and which will not,
Speak then to me, who neither beg nor fear
Your favours nor your hate. [I.iii]
Banquo asks the witches to see what the future holds

The Thane of Cawdor lives; why do you dress me
In borrowed robes? [I.iii]
*Macbeth cannot understand why Ross and Angus
address him as the Thane of Cawdor whom he knows to
be alive*

Oftentimes to win us to our harm,

The instruments of darkness tell us truths,
Win us with honest trifles, to betray's
In deepest consequence. [I.iii]
*Banquo is uneasy about the prophecies and where they
might lead*

This supernatural soliciting
Cannot be ill; cannot be good. If ill,
Why hath it given me earnest of success,
Commencing in a truth? I am Thane of Cawdor.
If good, why do I yield to that suggestion
Whose horrid image doth unfix my hair
And make my seated heart knock at my ribs
Against the use of nature? Present fears
Are less than horrible imaginings.
My thought, whose murder yet is but fantastical,
Shakes so my single state of man
That function is smother'd in surmise,
And nothing is but what is not. [I.iii]
*Macbeth has just received the title of Thane of Cawdor
giving credence to the witches' words. He is afraid where
they will lead him*

Malcolm: Nothing in his life
Became him like the leaving it: he died
As one that had been studied in his death
To throw away the dearest thing he ow'd
As 'twere a careless trifle.

Duncan: There's no art
To find the mind's construction in the face.
He was a gentleman on whom I built
An absolute trust. [I.iv]
Malcolm and Duncan discussing the death of the traitorous Thane of Cawdor

Glamis thou art, and Cawdor; and shalt be
What thou art promis'd. Yet do I fear thy nature;
It is too full o' th' milk of human kindness
To catch the nearest way. Thou wouldst be great;
Art not without ambition, but without
The illness should attend it. What thou wouldst
highly,
That wouldst thou holily; wouldst not play false,
And yet wouldst wrongly win.
Thou'dst have, great Glamis, that which cries
'Thus thou must do' if thou have it;
And that which rather thou dost fear to do
Than wishest should be undone. Hie thee hither,
That I may pour my spirits in thine ear,
And chastise with the valour of my tongue
All that impedes thee from the golden round
Which fate and metaphysical aid doth seem
To have thee crown'd withal. [I.v]
Lady Macbeth, having just received news of the prophecies, is determined that Macbeth's honesty and lack of ambition should not get in the way of his becoming king

The raven himself is hoarse
That croaks the fatal entrance of Duncan
Under my battlements. Come, you spirits
That tend on mortal thoughts, unsex me here;
And fill me, from the crown to the toe, top full
Of direst cruelty. Make thick my blood,
Stop up th' access and passage to remorse,
That no compunctious visitings of nature
Shake my fell purpose nor keep peace between
Th' effect and it. Come to my woman's breasts,
And take my milk for gall, you murd'ring ministers,
Wherever in your sightless substances
You wait on nature's mischief. Come, thick night,
And pall thee in the dunnest smoke of hell,
That my keen knife see not the wound it makes,
Nor heaven peep through the blanket of the dark
To cry 'Hold, hold.' [I.v]
Lady Macbeth, on hearing news of the King's approach,
asks for the strength of will to carry out his murder

Your face, my thane, is as a book where men
May read strange matters. To beguile the time,
Look like the time; bear welcome in your eye,
Your hand, your tongue; look like th' innocent
flower,
But be the serpent under't. [I.v]
Lady Macbeth advises Macbeth how to greet the King

If it were done when 'tis done, then 'twere well
It were done quickly. If th' assassination
Could trammel up the consequence, and catch,
With his surcease, success; that but this blow
Might be the be-all and the end-all here,
But here, upon this bank and shoal of time,
We'd jump the life to come. But in these cases
We still have judgment here, that we but teach
Bloody instructions, which being taught return
To plague th' inventor. This even-handed justice
Commends th' ingredience of our poison'd chalice
To our own lips. [I.vii]
*Macbeth is worrying about committing the murder and
what will happen to him in the afterlife*

Besides, this Duncan
Hath borne his faculties so meek, hath been
So clear in his great office, that his virtues
Will plead like angels, trumpet-tongu'd, against
The deep damnation of his taking-off;
And pity, like a naked new-born babe,
Striding the blast, or heaven's cherubin hors'd
Upon the sightless couriers of the air,
Shall blow the horrid deed in every eye,
That tears shall drown the wind. I have no spur
To prick the sides of my intent, but only

Vaulting ambition, which o'er-leaps itself,
And falls on th' other. [I.vii]
Macbeth knows what a good man King Duncan is.
Therefore to kill him is an even more atrocious crime

We will proceed no further in this business.
He hath honour'd me of late; and I have bought
Golden opinions from all sorts of people. [I.vii]
Macbeth wants to back out of the murder plan

Was the hope drunk
Wherein you dress'd yourself? Hath it slept since,
And wakes it now to look so green and pale
At what it did so freely? From this time
Such I account thy love. Art thou afeard
To be the same in thine own act and valour
As thou art in desire? Wouldst thou have that
Which thou esteem'st the ornament of life,
And live a coward in thine own esteem,
Letting 'I dare not' wait upon 'I would',
Like the poor cat i' th' adage? [I.vii]
Lady Macbeth mocks her husband and arouses his ambi-
tion with her cutting tongue

I dare do all that may become a man;
Who dares do more is none. [I.vii]
Macbeth on true manliness lying in virtue rather than
excess

Lady Macbeth: I have given suck, and know
How tender 'tis to love the babe that milks me:
I would, while it was smiling in my face,
Have pluck'd my nipple from his boneless gums,
And dash'd the brains out, had I so sworn
As you have done to this.
Macbeth: If we should fail?
Lady Macbeth: We fail!
But screw your courage to the sticking place,
And we'll not fail. [I.vii]
*Lady Macbeth reveals to what lengths she would go to
get what she wants*

False face must hide what the false heart doth
know. [I.vii]
Macbeth resolves to go ahead

Is this a dagger which I see before me,
The handle toward my hand? Come, let me clutch
thee.
I have thee not, and yet I see thee still.
Art thou not, fatal vision, sensible
To feeling as to sight? or art thou but
A dagger of the mind, a false creation,
Proceeding from the heat-oppressed brain?
[II.i]
Macbeth has hallucinations of a bloody dagger

Now o'er the one half-world
Nature seems dead, and wicked dreams abuse
The curtain'd sleep; now witchcraft celebrates
Pale Hecate's offerings; and wither'd murder,
Alarum'd by his sentinel, the wolf,
Whose howl's his watch, thus with his stealthy pace,
With Tarquin's ravishing strides, towards his design
Moves like a ghost. Thou sure and firm-set earth,
Hear not my steps which way they walk, for fear
Thy very stones prate of my whereabout
And take the present horror from the time,
Which now suits with it. Whiles I threat, he lives;
Words to the heat of deeds too cold breath gives.
I go, and it is done; the bell invites me.
Hear it not, Duncan, for it is a knell
That summons thee to heaven or to hell. [II.i]
Macbeth summons up the courage to go and kill the King

Had he not resembled
My father as he slept, I had done't. [II.ii]
*Lady Macbeth was unable to commit the murder herself
because the King looked like her father*

Methought I heard a voice cry 'Sleep no more;
Macbeth does murder sleep' – the innocent sleep,
Sleep that knits up the ravell'd sleave of care,
The death of each day's life, sore labour's bath,

Balm of hurt minds, great nature's second course,
Chief nourisher in life's feast. [II.ii]
Macbeth, on murdering the King, thought he heard a
voice prophesying that he would never sleep again

'Glamis hath murder'd sleep; and therefore Cawdor
Shall sleep no more. Macbeth shall sleep no more'.
[II.ii]
The prophecy Macbeth hears on murdering the king

Macbeth: I am afraid to think what I have done;
Look on't again I dare not.
Lady Macbeth: Infirm of purpose!
Give me the daggers. The sleeping and the dead
Are but as pictures; 'tis the eye of childhood
That fears a painted devil. If he do bleed,
I'll gild the faces of the grooms withal,
For it must seem their guilt. [II.ii]
Macbeth will not return to the King's chamber. Lady
Macbeth says she will return the daggers

Will all great Neptune's ocean wash this blood
Clean from my hand? No; this my hand will rather
The multitudinous seas incarnadine,
Making the green one red. [II.ii]
Macbeth is afraid no amount of water will wash the blood
from his hands

154

A little water clears us of this deed. [II.ii]
Lady Macbeth tells her husband to go and wash his
hands and there will be no evidence to incriminate them

The night has been unruly. Where we lay,
Our chimneys were blown down; and, as they say,
Lamentings heard i' th' air, strange screams of death,
And prophesying, with accents terrible,
Of dire combustion and confus'd events
New hatch'd to th' woeful time; the obscure bird
Clamour'd the livelong night. Some say the earth
Was feverous and did shake. [II.iii]
Lennox commenting on the wild night. He does not know
the King has been murdered

O horror, horror, horror! Tongue nor heart
Cannot conceive nor name thee. [II.iii]
Macduff has found the King's body

Shake off this downy sleep, death's counterfeit,
And look on death itself. Up, up, and see
The great doom's image! [II.iii]
Macduff arouses the household to see the King's body

Who can be wise, amaz'd, temp'rate, and furious,
Loyal and neutral, in a moment? No man. [II.iii]
Macbeth says that his reason for killing the guards out-
side the King's chamber had been fury

155

Where we are,
There's daggers in men's smiles; the near in blood,
The nearer bloody. [II.iii]
Malcolm and Donalbain resolve to flee the country in
fear of being accused of the King's murder

Thou hast it now: King, Cawdor, Glamis, all
As the weird women promis'd; and I fear
Thou play'dst most foully for't. [III.i]
Banquo suspects that Macbeth has been instrumental in
bringing about the witches' prophecies

Second Murderer: I am one, my liege,
Whom the vile blows and buffets of the world
Hath so incens'd, that I am reckless what
I do to spite the world.
First Murderer: And I another,
So weary with disasters, tugg'd with fortune,
That I would set my life on any chance,
To mend it or be rid on't. [III.i]
Macbeth enlists the help of two men to murder Banquo

Nought's had, all's spent,
Where our desire is got without content.
'Tis safer to be that which we destroy,
Than by destruction dwell in doubtful joy. [III.ii]
Lady Macbeth realising the need to eliminate any threat
that might expose them

Lady Macbeth: Things without all remedy
Should be without regard. What's done is done.
Macbeth: We have scotch'd the snake, not killed it;
She'll close, and be herself, whilst our poor malice
Remains in danger of her former tooth.
But let the frame of things disjoint, both the worlds
suffer,
Ere we will eat our meal in fear and sleep
In the affliction of these terrible dreams
That shake us nightly. Better be with the dead,
Whom we, to gain our peace, have sent to peace,
Than on the torture of the mind to lie
In restless ecstasy. Duncan is in his grave;
After life's fitful fever he sleeps well;
Treason has done his worst; nor steel, nor poison,
Malice domestic, foreign levy, nothing,
Can touch him further. [III.ii]
*Macbeth tries not to worry even though he knows he has
ample cause, and contrasts himself with Duncan who is
at peace*

Ere the bat hath flown
His cloister'd flight; ere to black Hecate's summons
The shard-borne beetle with his drowsy hums
Hath rung night's yawning peal, there shall be done
A deed of dreadful note. [III.ii]
Macbeth referring to the murder of Banquo

157

Light thickens, and the crow
Makes wing to th' rooky wood;
Good things of day begin to droop and drowse;
Whiles night's black agents to their preys do rouse.
[III.ii]
Macbeth on the coming of night

But now I am cabin'd, cribb'd, confin'd, bound in
To saucy doubts and fears. [III.iv]
Macbeth has heard of Banquo's death, but also that
Fleance, Banquo's son, has escaped

Hence, horrible shadow!
Unreal mock'ry, hence! [III.iv]
Macbeth sees the ghost of Banquo

Stand not upon the order of your going,
But go at once. [III.iv]
Lady Macbeth, realising her husband sees something
frightful, dismisses the banquet guests

I am in blood
Stepp'd in so far that, should I wade no more,
Returning were as tedious as go o'er. [III.iv]
Macbeth realises the extent of his crimes and how there is
no turning back

Round about the cauldron go;
In the poison'd entrails throw.
Toad that under cold stone

Days and nights has thirty-one
Swelt'red venom sleeping got
Boil thou first i' th' charmed pot.
Double, double toil and trouble;
Fire burn, and cauldron bubble. [IV.i]
The three witches

Eye of newt, and toe of frog,
Wool of bat, and tongue of dog,
Adder's fork, and blind-worm's sting,
Lizard's leg, and howlet's wing –
For a charm of pow'rful trouble,
Like a hell-broth boil and bubble. [IV.i]
The three witches

Second Witch: By the pricking of my thumbs,
Something wicked this way comes.
Open, locks, whoever knocks.
Macbeth: How now, you secret, black, and midnight
hags!
What is't you do?
Witches: A deed without a name. [IV.i]
Macbeth has gone to consult the witches

Be bloody, bold, and resolute; laugh to scorn
The pow'r of man, for none of woman born
Shall harm Macbeth. [IV.i]
The witches' first prophecy

Macbeth shall never vanquish'd be until
Great Birnam wood to high Dunsinane Hill
Shall come against him. [IV.i]
The witches' second prophecy

Malcolm: Let's make us med'cines of our great
revenge
To cure this deadly grief.
Macduff: He has no children. All my pretty ones?
Did you say all? O hell-kite! All?
What, all my pretty chickens and their dam
At one fell swoop? [IV.iii]
Macduff on learning that Macbeth has killed his family

Doctor: You see her eyes are open.
Gentlewoman: Ay, but their sense is shut. [V.i]
Lady Macbeth is sleepwalking

Out, damned spot! out, I say! One, two; why then
'tis time to do't. Hell is murky! Fie, my lord, fie! a
soldier, and afeard? What need we fear who knows
it, when none can call our pow'r to account? Yet
who would have thought the old man to have had
so much blood in him? [V.i]
*Lady Macbeth is trying to clean her hands. She thinks
she can see blood on them*

Here's the smell of the blood still. All the perfumes
of Arabia will not sweeten this little hand. Oh, oh,
oh! [V.i]
*Lady Macbeth is obsessed with removing the blood from
her hands*

Foul whisp'rings are abroad. Unnatural deeds
Do breed unnatural troubles; infected minds
To their deaf pillows will discharge their secrets.
More needs she the divine than the physician. [V.i]
*The Doctor realises that terrrible deeds have been com-
mitted and he can do nothing to cure Lady Macbeth's
psychological state*

Bring me no more reports; let them fly all.
Till Birnam wood remove to Dunsinane
I cannot taint with fear. [V.iii]
Macbeth feels safe because of the prophecy

I have liv'd long enough. My way of life
Is fall'n into the sear, the yellow leaf;
And that which should accompany old age,
As honour, love, obedience, troops of friends,
I must not look to have; but, in their stead,
Curses, not loud but deep, mouth-honour, breath,
Which the poor heart would fain deny, and dare
not. [V.iii]
Macbeth laments the life he has brought upon himself

Macbeth: Canst thou not minister to a mind diseas'd,
Pluck from the memory a rooted sorrow,
Raze out the written troubles of the brain,
And with some sweet oblivious antidote
Cleanse the stuff'd bosom of that perilous stuff
Which weighs upon the heart?
Doctor: Therein the patient
Must minister to himself.
Macbeth: Throw physic to the dogs – I'll none of it.
[V.iii]
Macbeth is angry because the Doctor cannot cure his wife

I have almost forgot the taste of fears.
The time has been my senses would have cool'd
To hear a night-shriek, and my fell of hair
Would at a dismal treatise rouse and stir
As life were in't. I have supp'd full with horrors;
Direness, familiar to my slaughterous thoughts,
Cannot once start me. [V.v]
*Macbeth, numbed, is no longer afraid. He has committed
so much evil nothing can scare him*

She should have died hereafter;
There would have been a time for such a word.
To-morrow, and to-morrow, and to-morrow,
Creeps in this petty pace from day to day
To the last syllable of recorded time,
And all our yesterdays have lighted fools

The way to dusty death. Out, out, brief candle!
Life's but a walking shadow, a poor player,
That struts and frets his hour upon the stage,
And then is heard no more; it is a tale
Told by an idiot, full of sound and fury,
Signifying nothing. [V.v]
Macbeth on hearing of his wife's death, reflects on life

As I did stand my watch upon the hall
I look'd toward Birnam, and anon me-thought
The wood began to move. [V.v]
*Messenger reporting on what he has seen. The prophecy
is fulfilled*

Macbeth: I bear a charmed life, which must not yield
To one of woman born.
Macduff: Despair thy charm;
And let the angel whom thou still hast serv'd
Tell thee Macduff was from his mother's womb
Untimely ripp'd. [V.viii]
*The other prophecy is fulfilled. Macduff was born by
Cæsarian section*

Lay on, Macduff;
And damn'd be him that first cries `Hold, enough!'
[V.viii]
*Macbeth resolved to fight to death rather than yield to
Malcolm as king*

Othello

Written 1603-4
Time and place of action Renaissance Venice and
Cyprus

> *Desdemona, a young Venetian girl, marries
> Othello, a much older Moorish general. Her father
> is incensed and publicly renounces his daughter.
> Iago, Othello's ensign, is jealous of young Cassio
> who has been made Othello's lieutenant. In order
> to get revenge he plans to make Othello insanely
> jealous by convincing his trusting master that
> Desdemona is having an affair with Cassio. Once
> convinced, Othello plans to kill Cassio and mur-
> ders Desdemona with his own hands. Iago's wife,
> Emilia, who is Desdemona's servant, reveals her
> husband's evil intention and her mistress' inno-
> cence. Othello, stricken with remorse at murder-
> ing his blameless young wife, stabs himself.*

We cannot all be masters, nor all masters
Cannot be truly follow'd. You shall mark

Many a duteous and knee-crooking knave
That, doting on his own obsequious bondage,
Wears out his time, much like his master's ass,
For nought but provender; and when he's old,
cashier'd.
Whip me such honest knaves. Others there are
Who, trimm'd in forms and visages of duty,
Keep yet their hearts attending on themselves;
And, throwing but shows of service on their lords,
Do well thrive by 'em and, when they have lin'd
their coats,
Do themselves homage – these fellows have some
soul;
And such a one do I profess myself.
For, sir,
It is as sure as you are Roderigo,
Were I the Moor, I would not be Iago.
In following him I follow but myself –
Heaven is my judge, not I for love and duty,
But seeming so for my peculiar end.
For when my outward action doth demonstrate
The native act and figure of my heart
In compliment extern, 'tis not long after
But I will wear my heart upon my sleeve
For daws to peck at: I am not what I am. [I.i]
*Iago to Roderigo on serving a master and his own
relationship with Othello*

Keep up your bright swords, for the dew will rust them. [I.ii]
Othello forestalling violence when confronted by Desdemona's father and his men

I'll refer me to all things of sense,
If she in chains of magic were not bound,
Whether a maid so tender, fair, and happy,
So opposite to marriage that she shunn'd
The wealthy curled darlings of our nation,
Would ever have, to incur a general mock,
Run from her guardage to the sooty bosom
Of such a thing as thou. [I.ii]
Desdemona's father, Brabantio, accuses Othello of bewitching his daughter into marrying him

And often did beguile her of her tears,
When I did speak of some distressful stroke
That my youth suffer'd. My story being done,
She gave me for my pains a world of sighs;
She swore, in faith, 'twas strange, 'twas passing strange;
'Twas pitiful, 'twas wondrous pitiful.
She wish'd she had not heard it, yet she wish'd
That heaven had made her such a man. She thank'd me;
And bade me, if I had a friend that lov'd her,
I should but teach him how to tell my story,

And that would woo her. Upon this hint I spake;
She lov'd me for the dangers I had pass'd;
And I lov'd her that she did pity them.
This only is the witchcraft I have us'd. [I.iii]
Othello recounts how Desdemona fell in love with him
through listening to all his exploits

I do perceive here a divided duty:
To you I am bound for life and education;
My life and education both do learn me
How to respect you; you are the lord of duty –
I am hitherto your daughter; but here's my husband,
And so much duty as my mother show'd
To you, preferring you before her father,
So much I challenge that I may profess
Due to the Moor, my lord. [I.iii]
Desdemona, to her father, on her loyalty to her husband

The tyrant custom, most grave senators,
Hath made the flinty and steel couch of war
My thrice-driven bed of down. [I.iii]
Othello is ready to go and fight the Turks as requested

If I be left behind,
A moth of peace, and he go to the war,
The rites for why I love him are bereft me,
And I a heavy interim shall support
By his dear absence. Let me go with him. [I.iii]
Desdemona asks to accompany her new husband

He hath a person and a smooth dispose
To be suspected, fram'd to make women false.
The Moor is of a free and open nature
That thinks men honest that but seem to be so. [I.iii]
Iago on Othello's trusting, almost naive, nature

Othello: It gives me wonder great as my content
To see you here before me. O my soul's joy!
If after every tempest come such calms,
May the winds blow till they have waken'd death,
And let the labouring bark climb hills of seas
Olympus-high and duck again as low
As hell's from heaven. If it were now to die,
'Twere now to be most happy; for I fear
My soul hath her content so absolute
That not another comfort like to this
Succeeds in unknown fate.
Desdemona: The heavens forbid
But that our loves and comforts should increase
Even as our days do grow! [II.i]
*Othello and Desdemona meeting after the separation of
the sea-journey*

Make the Moor thank me, love me, and reward me,
For making him egregiously an ass,
And practising upon his peace and quiet
Even to madness. [II.i]
Iago's plan to make Othello believe his wife is unfaithful

I have very poor and unhappy brains for drinking; I
could well wish courtesy would invent some other
custom of entertainment. [II.iii]
Cassio to Iago on his lack of head for drink

O God, that men should put an enemy in their
mouths to steal away their brains! That we should
with joy, pleasance, revel and applause, transform
ourselves into beasts! [II.iii]
*Cassio laments the fact that alcohol turns men into no
better than beasts*

Good name in man and woman, dear my lord,
Is the immediate jewel of their souls:
Who steals my purse steals trash; 'tis something,
nothing;
'Twas mine, 'tis his, and has been slave to thou-
sands;
But he that filches from me my good name
Robs me of that which not enriches him
And makes me poor indeed. [III.iii]
Iago to Othello on the importance of reputation

O, beware, my lord, of jealousy;
It is the green-ey'd monster which doth mock
The meat it feeds on. [III.iii]
Iago to Othello, about to sow the seeds of doubt

Look to your wife; observe her well with Cassio;
Wear your eyes thus, not jealous nor secure.
I would not have your free and noble nature
Our of self-bounty be abus'd; look to't.
I know our country disposition well:
In Venice they do let God see the pranks
They dare not show their husbands; their best con-
science
Is not to leave't undone, but keep't unknown.
[III.iii]
Iago tells Othello to watch Desdemona with Cassio

If I do prove her haggard,
Though that her jesses were my dear heart-strings,
I'd whistle her off and let her down the wind
To prey at fortune. Haply, for I am black
And have not those soft parts of conversation
That chamberers have, or for I am declin'd
Into the vale of years – yet that's not much –
She's gone; I am abus'd; and my relief
Must be to loathe her. O curse of marriage,
That we can call these delicate creatures ours,
And not their appetites! I had rather be a toad,
And live upon the vapour of a dungeon,
Than keep a corner in the thing I love
For others' uses. [III.iii]
Othello is afraid that Desdemona has been unfaithful
because of his colour or age

Trifles light as air
Are to the jealous confirmations strong
As proofs of holy writ. [III.iii]
*Iago realises that he has successfully planted the seeds of
jealousy in Othello's mind*

Not poppy, nor mandragora,
Nor all the drowsy syrups of the world,
Shall ever medicine thee to that sweet sleep
Which thou owed'st yesterday. [III.iii]
Iago enjoying idea that Othello will no longer sleep sweetly

I had been happy if the general camp,
Pioneers and all, had tasted her sweet body,
So I had nothing known. O, now for ever
Farewell the tranquil mind! farewell content!
Farewell the plumed troops and the big wars
That makes ambition virtue! O, farewell!
Farewell the neighing steed and the shrill trump,
The spirit-stirring drum, th' ear-piercing fife,
The royal banner, and all quality,
Pride, pomp, and circumstance, of glorious war!
And O you mortal engines whose rude throats
Th' immortal Jove's dread clamours counterfeit,
Farewell! Othello's occupation's gone. [III.iii]
*Othello to Iago, stating that he could have borne
Desdemona's unfaithfulness if he had known nothing
about it. Now he has lost his peace of mind forever*

Like to the Pontic sea,
Whose icy current and compulsive course
Ne'er feels retiring ebb, but keeps due on
To the Propontic and the Hellespont;
Even so my bloody thoughts, with violent pace,
Shall ne'er look back, ne'er ebb to humble love,
Till that a capable and wide revenge
Swallow them up. [III.iii]
Othello vows vengeance

'Tis true. There's magic in the web of it.
A sibyl that had numb'red in the world
The sun to course two hundred compasses
In her prophetic fury sew'd the work;
The worms were hallowed that did breed the silk;
And it was dy'd in mummy which the skilful
Conserv'd of maidens' hearts. [III.iv]
*Othello is desciding the handkerchief given to him by his
mother and which he gave to Desdemona*

Jealous souls will not be answer'd so;
They are not ever jealous for the cause,
But jealous for they are jealous. 'Tis a monster
Begot upon it self, born on it self. [III.iv]
Emilia to Desdemona on the nature of jealousy

Work on,
My medicine, work. Thus credulous fools are caught;

And many worthy and chaste dames even thus,
All guiltless, meet reproach. [IV.i]
Iago on the ease with which lies will be believed

My heart is turn'd to stone; I strike it, and it hurts
my hand. O, the world hath not a sweeter creature;
she might lie by an emperor's side and command
him tasks. [IV.i]
Othello is convinced of Desdemona's adultery

Is this the nature
Whom passion could not shake, whose solid virtue
The shot of accident nor dart of chance
Could neither graze nor pierce? [IV.i]
Lodovico on the change in Othello from a level-headed
man to somebody who strikes his wife

Had it pleas'd heaven
To try me with affliction; had they rain'd
All kind of sores and shames on my bare head,
Steep'd me in poverty to the very lips,
Given to captivity me and my utmost hopes,
I should have found in some place of my soul
A drop of patience; but, alas, to make me
The fixed figure for the time of scorn
To point his slow unmoving finger at! O, O!
Yet could I bear that too; well, very well;
But there, where I have garner'd up my heart,

Where either I must live or bear no life,
The fountain from the which my current runs,
Or else dries up; to be discarded thence!
Or keep it as a cistern for foul toads
To knot and gender in! Turn thy complexion there,
Patience, thou young and rose-lipp'd cherubin;
Ay, here, look grim as hell! [IV.ii]
Othello accusing Desdemona of cuckolding him

I cry you mercy, then.
I took you for that cunning whore of Venice
That married with Othello. – You, mistress,
That have the office opposite to Saint Peter
And keeps the gate of hell! [IV.ii]
*Othello accusing Desdemona of being unfaithful and of
treating Emilia as her bawd*

Emilia: I would you had never seen him.
Desdemona: So would not I: my love doth so
approve him
That even his stubbornness, his checks, his frowns –
Prithee unpin me – Have grace and favour in them.
[IV.iii]
Desdemona's love is all-embracing

But I do think it is their husbands' faults
If wives do fall. Say that they slack their duties,
And pour our treasures into foreign laps;

Or else break out in peevish jealousies,
Throwing restraint upon us; or say they strike us,
Or scant our former having in despite;
Why, we have galls; and though we have some grace,
Yet have we some revenge. Let husbands know
Their wives have sense like them; they see and smell,
And have their palates both for sweet and sour
As husbands have. What is it that they do
When they change us for others? Is it sport?
I think it is. And doth affection breed it?
I think it doth. Is't frailty that thus errs?
It is so too. And have not we affections,
Desires for sport, and frailty, as men have?
Then let them use us well; else let them know
The ills we do their ills instruct us so. [IV.iii]
Emilia talking of wives and adultery

It is the cause, it is the cause, my soul –
Let me not name it to you, you chaste stars! –
It is the cause. Yet I'll not shed her blood,
Nor scar that whiter skin of hers than snow,
And smooth as monumental alabaster.
Yet she must die, else she'll betray more men.
Put out the light, and then put out the light.
If I quench thee, thou flaming minister,
I can again thy former light restore,
Should I repent me, but once put out thy light,
Thou cunning'st pattern of excelling nature,

I know not where is that Promethean heat
That can thy light relume. When I have pluck'd thy rose,
I cannot give it vital growth again;
It needs must wither. I'll smell it on the tree.
                              [Kissing her
O balmy breath, that dost almost persuade
Justice to break her sword! One more, one more.
Be thus when thou art dead, and I will kill thee,
And love thee after. One more, and that's the last:
So sweet was ne'er so fatal. I must weep,
But they are cruel tears. This sorrow's heavenly;
It strikes where it doth love. [V.ii]
Othello determines to kill the sleeping Desdemona

Alas, why gnaw you so your nether lip?
Some bloody passion shakes your very frame.
These are portents; but yet, I hope, I hope,
They do not point on me. [V.ii]
Desdemona is afraid of Othello's strange behaviour

Othello: She's like a liar gone to burning hell:
'Twas I that kill'd her.
Emilia: O, the more angel she,
And you the blacker devil! [V.ii]
Desdemona has just expired, saying that she herself was responsible for her death

Nay, had she been true,
If heaven would make me such another world
Of one entire and perfect chrysolite,
I'd not have sold her for it. [V.ii]
Othello would have prized a faithful Desdemona above all worth

O thou dull Moor! That handkerchief thou speak'st of
I found by fortune, and did give my husband;
For often with a solemn earnestness –
More than indeed belong'd to such a trifle –
He begg'd me to steal it. [V.ii]
Emilia is telling Othello that she found the handkerchief which he believed Desdemona had given to Cassio

O ill-starr'd wench!
Pale as thy smock! When we shall meet at compt,
This look of thine will hurl my soul from heaven,
And fiends will snatch at it. Cold, cold, my girl!
Even like thy chastity. O cursed, cursed slave!
Whip me, ye devils,
From the possession of this heavenly sight.
Blow me about in winds, roast me in sulphur,
Wash me in steep-down gulfs of liquid fire.
O Desdemona! Dead! Desdemona! Dead! [V.ii]
Othello realises that he has killed his innocent wife

An honourable murderer, if you will;
For nought I did in hate, but all in honour. [V.ii]
Othello tries to justify his killing of Desdemona

I have done the state some service, and they know't;
No more of that. I pray you, in your letters,
When you shall these unlucky deeds relate,
Speak of me as I am; nothing extenuate,
Nor set down aught in malice. Then must you speak
Of one that lov'd not wisely, but too well;
Of one not easily jealous, but, being wrought,
Perplexed in the extreme; of one whose hand,
Like the base Indian, threw a pearl away
Richer than all his tribe; of one whose subdu'd eyes
Albeit unused to the melting mood,
Drops tears as fast as the Arabian trees
Their med'cinable gum. Set you down this:
And say besides that in Aleppo once,
Where a malignant and a turban'd Turk
Beat a Venetian and traduc'd the state,
I took by th' throat the circumcised dog,
And smote him thus. [V.ii]
Othello asks not to be judged too harshly after his death.
He was driven to jealousy. He stabs himself

Gratiano: All that is spoke is marr'd.
Othello: I kiss'd thee ere I kill'd thee. No way but this,
Killing my self, to die upon a kiss. [V.ii]
Othello stabbing himself, falls beside Desdemona

Pericles, Prince of Tyre

Written 1608-9
Time and place of action Hellenistic period, the
Eastern Mediterranean

*Pericles flees Antioch because he discovers King
Antiochus' incestuous affair with his daughter.
Shipwrecked off Pentapolis, Pericles is welcomed
by King Simonides who invites him to take part
in a tournament. Pericles wins the heart of
Thaisa, Simonides' daughter. They marry and
when Pericles hears of King Antiochus' death he
returns to Tyre, but during the journey home it
appears that Thaisa dies giving birth and is cast
ashore in a casket. She is resuscitated and enters
the Temple of Diana. Pericles gives his daughter,
Marina, into the care of a couple who bring her up
until she is kidnapped by pirates and taken to a
brothel in Mytilene. She is eventually reunited
with her father. In a vision the Goddess Diana
summons them and they are reunited with Thaisa.*

See where she comes, apparell'd like the spring,
Graces her subjects, and her thoughts the king
Of every virtue gives renown to men. [I.i]
Pericles on seeing the daughter of Antiochus

'Tis time to fear, when tyrants seem to kiss. [I.ii]
*Pericles to Helicanus, concerning Antiochus' smooth
attitude toward him*

3rd Fisherman: I marvel how the fishes live in the
sea.
1st Fisherman: Why, as men do a-land – the great
ones eat up the little ones. [II.i]
Fishermen philosophising

Opinion's but a fool, that makes us scan
The outward habit by the inward man. [II.ii]
*Simonides to his lords, who had spoken of Pericles' shab-
by appearance*

Thou god of this great vast, rebuke these surges,
Which wash both heaven and hell; and thou that
hast
Upon the winds command, bind them in brass,
Having call'd them from the deep! O, still
Thy deaf'ning dreadful thunders; gently quench
Thy nimble sulphurous flashes! ...

The seaman's whistle
Is as a whisper in the ears of death,
Unheard. [III.i]
Pericles during a storm at sea

A terrible childbed hast thou had, my dear;
No light, no fire. Th' unfriendly elements
Forgot thee utterly; nor have I time
To give thee hallow'd to thy grave, but straight
Must cast thee, scarcely coffin'd, in the ooze;
Where, for a monument upon thy bones,
And aye-remaining lamps, the belching whale
And humming water must o'erwhelm thy corpse,
Lying with simple shells. [III.i]
Pericles believes his wife dead in childbirth during the storm at sea

Give me a gash, put me to present pain,
Lest this great sea of joys rushing upon me
O'erbear the shores of my mortality,
And drown me with their sweetness. O, come hither,
Thou that beget'st him that did thee beget;
Thou that wast born at sea, buried at Tharsus,
And found at sea again! [V.i]
Pericles on regaining his daughter Marina

Romeo and Juliet

Written 1595-6
Time and place of action 15th-Century Verona

Set against an ancient feud between two rival families, Romeo, a Montague, and Juliet, a Capulet, fall in love and secretly marry. Romeo is involved in a fight and kills Tybalt, a Capulet. He is banished. Juliet's parents, unaware of the secret marriage, arrange for her to marry Paris. Unable to turn to either her mother or nurse for help, Juliet goes to the Friar who married them. He arranges for her to drink a potion that will make her appear dead for forty-two hours and he sends word for Romeo to come and get her. The message Romeo receives is that she is dead. He goes to the tomb, kills the mourning Paris, and then poisons himself. When Juliet wakes and sees what has happened, she stabs herself. Their deaths bring the two families together.

Two households, both alike in dignity,
In fair Verona, where we lay our scene,

From ancient grudge break to new mutiny,
Where civil blood makes civil hands unclean.
From forth the fatal loins of these two foes
A pair of star-cross'd lovers take their life;
Whose misadventur'd piteous overthrows
Doth with their death bury their parents' strife.
The fearful passage of their death-mark'd love,
And the continuance of their parents' rage,
Which, but their children's end, nought could
remove,
Is now the two hours' traffic of our stage. [Prologue]

My child is yet a stranger in the world,
She hath not seen the change of fourteen years;
Let two more summers wither in their pride
Ere we may think her ripe to be a bride. [I.ii]
*Juliet's father, Capulet, responding to Paris' request to
marry her*

And then my husband – God be with his soul!
'A was a merry man – took up the child.
'Yea,' quoth he 'dost thou fall upon thy face?
Thou wilt fall backward when thou hast more wit,
Wilt thou not, Jule?' And, by my holidam,
The pretty wretch left crying, and said 'Ay' ...
And, pretty fool, it stinted, and said 'Ay'. [I.iii]
*Juliet's nurse reminiscing about Juliet as a child and her
husband's rather bawdy comments*

O, then I see Queen Mab hath been with you.
She is the fairies' midwife, and she comes
In shape no bigger than an agate stone
On the fore-finger of an alderman,
Drawn with a team of little atomies
Athwart men's noses as they lie asleep;
Her waggon-spokes made of long spinners' legs;
The cover, of the wings of grasshoppers;
Her traces, of the smallest spider's web;
Her collars, of the moonshine's wat'ry beams;
Her whip, of cricket's bone; the lash, of film;
Her waggoner, a small grey-coated gnat,
Not half so big as a round little worm
Prick'd from the lazy finger of a maid.
Her chariot is an empty hazel-nut,
Made by the joiner squirrel or old grub,
Time out o' mind the fairies' coachmakers.
And in this state she gallops night by night
Through lovers' brains, and then they dream of love;
O'er courtiers' knees, that dream on curtsies straight;
O'er lawyers' fingers, who straight dream on fees;
O'er ladies' lips, who straight on kisses dream,
Which oft the angry Mab with blisters plagues,
Because their breaths with sweetmeats tainted are.
Sometime she gallops o'er a courtier's nose,
And then dreams he of smelling out a suit;
And sometime comes she with a tithe-pig's tail,

Tickling a parson's nose as 'a lies asleep,
Then dreams he of another benefice.
Sometime she driveth o'er a soldier's neck,
And then dreams he of cutting foreign throats,
Of breaches, ambuscadoes, Spanish blades,
Of healths five fathom deep; and then anon
Drums in his ear, at which he starts and wakes,
And, being thus frighted, swears a prayer or two,
And sleeps again. This is that very Mab
That plats the manes of horses in the night;
And bakes the elf-locks in foul sluttish hairs,
Which once untangled much misfortune bodes.
This is the hag, when maids lie on their backs,
That presses them and learns them first to bear,
Making them women of good carriage. [I.iv]
Mercutio fantasising about the fairy queen

O, she doth teach the torches to burn bright!
It seems she hangs upon the cheek of night
As a rich jewel in an Ethiop's ear;
Beauty too rich for use, for earth too dear!
So shows a snowy dove trooping with crows
As yonder lady o'er her fellows shows.
The measure done, I'll watch her place of stand,
And, touching hers, make blessed my rude hand.
Did my heart love till now? Forswear it, sight;
For I ne'er saw true beauty till this night. [I.v]
Romeo falling in love on first sight with Juliet

But, soft! What light through yonder window breaks?
It is the east, and Juliet is the sun. [II.ii]
Romeo catching sight of Juliet on the balcony

See how she leans her cheek upon her hand!
O that I were a glove upon that hand,
That I might touch that cheek! [II.ii]
Romeo watching Juliet on the balcony

O Romeo, Romeo! wherefore art thou Romeo?
Deny thy father and refuse thy name;
Or, if thou wilt not, be but sworn my love,
And I'll no longer be a Capulet. [II.ii]
*Juliet wishes Romeo could renounce his parentage, or if
that cannot be, that she could renounce her own*

What's in a name? That which we call a rose
By any other name would smell as sweet;
So Romeo would, were he not Romeo call'd,
Retain that dear perfection which he owes
Without that title. [II.ii]
Juliet wishes Romeo had a different name and parentage

With love's light wings did I o'er-perch these walls,
For stony limits cannot hold love out;
And what love can do, that dares love attempt. [II.ii]
*Romeo stating that love makes man bold enough to
attempt anything, even if it is dangerous*

Thou knowest the mask of night is on my face,
Else would a maiden blush bepaint my cheek
For that which thou hast heard me speak to-night.
Fain would I dwell on form, fain, fain deny
What I have spoke; but farewell compliment! [II.ii]
*Juliet fears that she has been too fast and forward in
declaring her love but does not regret it*

Romeo: Lady, by yonder blessed moon I vow,
That tips with silver all these fruit-tree tops –
Juliet: O, swear not by the moon, th' inconstant
moon,
That monthly changes in her circled orb,
Lest that thy love prove likewise variable.
Romeo: What shall I swear by?
Juliet: Do not swear at all;
Or, if thou wilt, swear by thy gracious self,
Which is the god of my idolatry. [II.ii]
Juliet and Romeo exchanging love vows

It is too rash, too unadvis'd, too sudden;
Too like the lightning, which doth cease to be
Ere one can say 'It lightens'. Sweet, good-night!
This bud of love, by summer's ripening breath,
May prove a beauteous flow'r when next we meet.
[II.ii]
*Juliet is fearful that their love is too sudden, but it may
mature at the next meeting*

My bounty is as boundless as the sea,
My love as deep: the more I give to thee,
The more I have, for both are infinite. [II.ii]
Juliet telling Romeo how much she loves him

Good-night, good-night! Parting is such sweet sorrow
That I shall say good night till it be morrow.
Romeo: Sleep dwell upon thine eyes, peace in thy
breast!
Would I were sleep and peace, so sweet to rest! [II.ii]
Romeo and Juliet saying goodnight to each other

Romeo: Courage, man; the hurt cannot be much.
Mercutio: No, 'tis not so deep as a well, nor so wide
as a church door, but 'tis enough, 'twill serve. Ask
for me tomorrow, and you shall find me a grave
man. I am peppered, I warrant, for this world. A
plague a both your houses! Zounds, a dog, a rat, a
mouse, a cat, to scratch a man to death! [III.i]
*Mercutio has been wounded in a fight with Tybalt and is
about to die*

Gallop apace, you fiery-footed steeds,
Towards Phoebus' lodging; such a waggoner
As Phaethon would whip you to the west,
And bring in cloudy night immediately.
Spread thy close curtain, love-performing night,

That runaways' eyes may wink, and Romeo
Leap to these arms, untalk'd of and unseen.
Lovers can see to do their amorous rites
By their own beauties; or if love be blind,
It best agrees with night. Come, civil night,
Thou sober-suited matron, all in black,
And learn me how to lose a winning match,
Play'd for a pair of stainless maidenhoods;
Hood my unmann'd blood, bating in my cheeks,
With thy black mantle, till strange love, grown bold,
Think true love acted simple modesty.
Come, night; come, Romeo; come, thou day in night;
For thou wilt lie upon the wings of night
Whiter than new snow on a raven's back.
Come, gentle night, come, loving, black-brow'd night,
Give me my Romeo; and, when he shall die,
Take him and cut him out in little stars,
And he will make the face of heaven so fine
That all the world will be in love with night,
And pay no worship to the garish sun.
O, I have bought the mansion of a love,
But not possess'd it; and though I am sold,
Not yet enjoy'd. So tedious is this day
As is the night before some festival
To an impatient child that hath new robes,
And may not wear them. [III.ii]

Juliet is impatient for Romeo and the consummation of
their love which for her is the pinnacle of their marriage

Romeo, come forth; come forth, thou fearful man;
Affliction is enamour'd of thy parts,
And thou art wedded to calamity. [III.iii]
Friar Lawrence is hiding Romeo in his cell

Thou canst not speak of that thou dost not feel.
Wert thou as young as I, Juliet thy love,
An hour but married, Tybalt murdered,
Doting like me, and like me banished,
Then mightst thou speak, then mightst thou tear thy
hair,
And fall upon the ground, as I do now,
Taking the measure of an unmade grave [III.iii]
*Romeo to Friar Lawrence saying that he cannot conceive
what he is going through*

Night's candles are burnt out, and jocund day
Stands tiptoe on the misty mountain tops.
I must be gone and live, or stay and die. [III.v]
Romeo has to leave Juliet because he has been banished

I pray you tell my lord and father, madam
I will not marry yet; and when I do, I swear
It shall be Romeo, whom you know I hate,
Rather than Paris. [III.v]
Juliet's parents want her to marry Paris

O, sweet my mother, cast me not away!
Delay this marriage for a month, a week;
Or, if you do not, make the bridal bed
In that dim monument where Tybalt lies. [III.v]
*Juliet beseeches her mother to delay the proposed wedding
to Paris*

Farewell! God knows when we shall meet again.
I have a faint cold fear thrills through my veins,
That almost freezes up the heat of life. [IV.iii]
*Juliet, about to take the drug, wonders when she will see
her parents again*

Out, alas! she's cold;
Her blood is settled, and her joints are stiff.
Life and these lips have long been separated.
Death lies on her like an untimely frost
Upon the sweetest flower of all the field. [IV.v]
*Capulet, on entering Juliet's chamber on the day of her
marriage*

How oft when men are at the point of death
Have they been merry! Which their keepers call
A lightning before death. O, how may I
Call this a lightning? O my love! My wife!
Death, that hath suck'd the honey of thy breath,

Hath had no power yet upon thy beauty.
Thou art not conquer'd; beauty's ensign yet
Is crimson in thy lips and in thy cheeks,
And death's pale flag is not advanced there.
Tybalt, liest thou there in thy bloody sheet?
O, what more favour can I do to thee
Than with that hand that cut thy youth in twain
To sunder his that was thine enemy?
Forgive me, cousin. Ah, dear Juliet,
Why art thou yet so fair? Shall I believe
That unsubstantial Death is amorous,
And that the lean abhorred monster keeps
Thee here in dark to be his paramour?
For fear of that I still will stay with thee,
And never from this palace of dim night
Depart again. Here, here will I remain
With worms that are thy chambermaids. O, here
Will I set up my everlasting rest,
And shake the yoke of inauspicious stars
From this world-wearied flesh. Eyes, look your last.
Arms, take your last embrace. And, lips, O you
The doors of breath, seal with a righteous kiss
A dateless bargain to engrossing death! [V.iii]
*Romeo says farewell to his dead wife and prepares to take
the poison*

Timon of Athens

Written 1607-8

Time and place of action Antiquity, Athens and
nearby wilderness

*Timon, through over-generosity to his so-called
friends, becomes bankrupt. When he asks these
friends for help, they all turn their backs on him.
Enraged with humanity in general, Timon with-
draws to the wilderness where he discovers gold.
His loyal steward, Flavius, goes in search of his
master and Timon acknowledges that there is at
least one good man in the world and gives him
gold. Alcibiades, a banished general, plans to
attack Athens. Timon is pleased and gives him
gold to pay the soldiers. Alcibiades takes Athens
and learns that Timon is dead.*

His large fortune,
Upon his good and gracious nature hanging,
Subdues and properties to his love and tendance
All sorts of hearts [I.i]
Poet talking of Timon's extravagant generosity

'Tis not enough to help the feeble up,
But to support him after. [I.i]
*Timon agrees to pay debts of Ventidius who turns out to
be a false friend*

You mistake my love;
I gave it freely ever; and there's none
Can truly say he gives, if he receives. [I.ii]
*Timon refuses to accept repayment of the debts by
Ventidius*

No care, no stop! So senseless of expense
That he will neither know how to maintain it
Nor cease his flow of riot; takes no account
How things go from him, nor resumes no care
Of what is to continue. Never mind
Was to be so unwise to be so kind. [II.ii]
*Flavius, Timon's steward, is worried about the mounting
bills*

And, in some sort, these wants of mine are crown'd
That I account them blessings; for by these
Shall I try friends. You shall perceive how you
Mistake my fortunes; I am wealthy in my friends.
[II.ii]
*Timon is confident that his friends will help him out with
his debts*

They have all been touch'd and found base metal, for
They have all denied him. [III.iii]
*Timon's servant to Sempronius, telling him that none of
Timon's so-called friends will lend him money*

Live loath'd and long,
Most smiling, smooth, detested parasites,
Courteous destroyers, affable wolves, meek bears,
You fools of fortune, trencher friends, time's flies,
Cap and knee slaves, vapours, and minute-jacks!
[III.vi]
*Timon rages against his former friends whom he has
invited to a false banquet*

Timon will to the woods, where he shall find
Th' unkindest beast more kinder than mankind. [IV.i]
Timon leaves Athens to go and live in the wilderness

I'll follow and enquire him out.
I'll ever serve his mind with my best will;
Whilst I have gold, I'll be his steward still. [IV.ii]
*Flavius, Timon's faithful steward, determines to seek him
out in the wilderness and carry on serving him*

The sun's a thief, and with his great attraction
Robs the vast sea; the moon's an arrant thief,
And her pale fire she snatches from the sun:

The sea's a thief, whose liquid surge resolves
The moon into salt tears; the earth's a thief,
That feeds and breeds by a composture stol'n
From gen'ral excrement – each thing's a thief.
[IV.iii]
Timon, grown cynical, sees theft everywhere

Surely, this man
Was born of woman.
Forgive my general and exceptless rashness,
You perpetual-sober gods! I do proclaim
One honest man – mistake me not, but one;
No more, I pray – and he's a steward. [IV.iii]
Timon acknowledges that Flavius, his steward, is a good man

Timon hath made his everlasting mansion
Upon the beached verge of the salt flood,
Who once a day with his embossed froth
The turbulent surge shall cover. [V.i]
Timon intends to make his grave by the sea's edge

Titus Andronicus

Written 1592-3
Time and place of action Early Christian era, Rome

*Titus Andronicus, victorious, returns to Rome
with his captives, Tamora, Queen of the Goths
and her three sons. Her eldest son is sacrificed.
Titus turns down the title of Emperor in favour of
Saturninus who promises to marry Lavinia, Titus'
daughter. Saturninus' brother Bassianus claims
Lavinia for himself and is supported by Titus'
sons. In a struggle Titus kills his youngest son.
Saturninus renounces Lavinia and marries
Tamora, who has a Moor lover, Aaron. Her sons
kill Bassianus and horribly rape and mutilate
Lavinia. They also kidnap two of Titus' sons.
Aaron convinces Titus that they will be returned
if he sends a hand in ransom. Titus does this but
receives it back accompanied by the heads of his
sons. Titus goes mad and engineers a gruesome
revenge involving baking the flesh of Tamora's
sons in a pie which she then eats, slaughtering his
daughter and then Tamora. Saturninus kills Titus*

and is in turn killed by Lucius, Titus' only remaining son.

For now I stand as one upon a rock,
Environ'd with a wilderness of sea,
Who marks the waxing tide grow wave by wave,
Expecting ever when some envious surge
Will in his brinish bowels swallow him. [III.i]

The eagle suffers little birds to sing,
And is not careful what they mean thereby. [IV.iv]
*Tamora to Saturninus, who has told her that the citizens
have been talking against him*

There they are, both baked in this pie,
Whereof their mother daintily hath fed,
Eating the flesh that she herself hath bred. [V.iii]
*Titus, dressed as a cook, has served Tamora's sons to her
baked in a pie*

Troilus and Cressida

Written 1601-2

Time and place of action Trojan War, Troy and the Greek camp

Troilus, a young prince of Troy, falls in love with Cressida whose father has deserted to the Greek camp. Engineered by her uncle, Pandarus, Troilus and Cressida become lovers. They are forced to part when Cressida is given in exchange to the Greeks for a Trojan soldier. Troilus gets the opportunity to visit Cressida but he finds her embracing Diomedes. Heartbroken, Troilus returns to Troy, whose doom is sealed with the slaughter of Hector by Achilles and his men.

I tell thee I am mad
In Cressid's love. Thou answer'st 'She is fair'–
Pourest in the open ulcer of my heart –
Her eyes, her hair, her cheek, her gait, her voice,
Handlest in thy discourse. O, that her hand,
In whose comparison all whites are ink

Writing their own reproach; to whose soft seizure
The cygnet's down is harsh, and spirit of sense
Hard as the palm of ploughman! [I.i]
*Troilus to Pandarus telling him how much he is in love
with Cressida*

How could communities,
Degrees in schools, and brotherhoods in cities,
Peaceful commerce from dividable shores,
The primogenity and due of birth,
Prerogative of age, crowns, sceptres, laurels,
But by degree, stand in authentic place?
Take but degree away, untune that string,
And hark what discord follows! Each thing melts
In mere oppugnancy...
Then everything includes itself in power,
Power into will, will into appetite;
And appetite, an universal wolf,
So doubly seconded with will and power,
Must make perforce an universal prey
and last eat up himself. [I.iii]
*Ulysses, on the need for order and respect. Otherwise
everything falls into chaos*

Cry, Troyans, cry. Practise your eyes with tears.
Troy must not be, nor goodly Ilion stand;
Our firebrand brother, Paris, burns us all.
Cry, Troyans, cry, A Helen and a woe!

Cry, cry. Troy burns, or else let Helen go. [II.ii]
Cassandra's prophecy

This is the monstruosity in love, lady, that the will
is infinite, and the execution confin'd; that the
desire is boundless, and the act a slave to limit. [III.ii]
Troilus to Cressida on the nature of love and passion

Time hath, my lord, a wallet at his back,
Wherein he puts alms for oblivion,
A great-siz'd monster of ingratitudes.
Those scraps are good deeds past, which are
devour'd
As fast as they are made, forgot as soon
As done. [III.iii]
Ulysses to Achilles saying the memory of good deeds
fades with time

Beauty, wit,
High birth, vigour of bone, desert in service,
Love, friendship, charity, are subjects all
To envious and calumniating Time.
One touch of nature makes the whole world kin,
That all with one consent praise new-born gawds,
Though they are made and moulded of things past,
And give to dust that is a little gilt
More laud than gilt o'er-dusted [III.iii]
Ulysses to Achilles on the universal desire for novelty

We two, that with so many thousand sighs
Did buy each other, must poorly sell ourselves
With the rude brevity and discharge of one.
Injurious time now with a robber's haste
Crams his rich thievery up, he knows not how.
As many farewells as be stars in heaven,
With distinct breath and consign'd kisses to them,
He fumbles up into a loose adieu,
And scants us with a single famish'd kiss,
Distasted with the salt of broken tears. [IV.iv]
Troilus to Cressida on her leaving for the Greek camp

Fie, fie upon her!
There's language in her eye, her cheek, her lip,
Nay, her foot speaks; her wanton spirits look out
At every joint and motive of her body. [IV.v]
Ulysses talking of Cressida's sexual forwardness

Lechery, lechery! Still wars and lechery! Nothing
else holds fashion. A burning devil take them! [V.ii]
Thersites' remark about wars and lechery

Hector is dead; there is no more to say. [V.x]
Troilus announces Hector's death

THE HISTORIES

King John

Written 1596
Time and place of action Beginning of 13th
Century, England and France

*King John's crown is at risk when Philip of France
and the Duke of Austria threaten war, demanding
that John's nephew, Arthur, take the English
throne. War is declared as John invades France.
Peace, achieved through the marriage of John's
niece, Blanch, to the Dauphin, is short-lived when
John is threatened with excommunication for dis-
obedience to the Pope, and Philip for his treacher-
ous pact. The battle resumes. England is victorious, and the Duke of Austria is killed by Richard
I's son, Philip the Bastard. Arthur is captured and
sent to England. Fearing execution, he dies in an
escape bid. John, suspected of Arthur's murder,
faces attack from the English nobility who join
the Dauphin in invading England. Having retired
to Swinstead Abbey, John is poisoned by a monk.*

*The English lords who have supported the
Dauphin then transfer their allegiance to Prince
Henry, who is crowned King Henry III. The play
closes with a patriotic speech by Philip the
Bastard.*

Hadst thou rather be a Faulconbridge,
And like thy brother, to enjoy thy land,
Or the reputed son of Coeur-de-lion,
Lord of thy presence and no land beside? [I.i]
Elinor, King John's mother, to Philip the Bastard

Courage mounteth with occasion. [II.i]
*The Duke of Austria to the King of France on their attack
against the English throne*

Zounds! I was never so bethump'd with words
Since I first call'd my brother's father dad. [II.i]
*Philip the Bastard, responding to the rhetoric of the
citizens of Angiers*

Bell, book, and candle, shall not drive me back,
When gold and silver becks me to come on. [III.iii]
*Philip the Bastard siding with King John against the
Pope's threat of excommunication*

Grief fills the room up of my absent child,
Lies in his bed, walks up and down with me,
Puts on his pretty looks, repeats his words,

Remembers me of all his gracious parts,
Stuffs out his vacant garments with his form;
Then have I reason to be fond of grief. [III.iv]
Lady Constance on the imprisonment of her son Arthur

Life is as tedious as a twice-told tale
Vexing the dull ear of a drowsy man. [III.iv]
The Dauphin depressed at the turn of events

I will not struggle, I will stand stone-still.
For heaven sake, Hubert, let me not be bound!
Nay, hear me, Hubert! Drive these men away,
And I will sit as quiet as a lamb;
I will not stir, nor wince, nor speak a word,
Nor look upon the iron angrily. [IV.i]
*Hubert has come to put Arthur's eyes out. Arthur asks
him to send the executioners away*

To be possess'd with double pomp,
To guard a title that was rich before,
To gild refined gold, to paint the lily,
To throw a perfume on the violet,
To smooth the ice, or add another hue
Unto the rainbow, or with taper-light
To seek the beauteous eye of heaven to garnish,
Is wasteful and ridiculous excess. [IV.ii]
*Salisbury to the King referring to a second coronation as
wasteful expense*

Heaven take my soul, and England keep my bones!
[IV.iii]
Arthur falls to his death trying to escape from the castle

None of you will bid the winter come
To thrust his icy fingers in my maw,
Nor let my kingdom's rivers take their course
Through my burn'd bosom, nor entreat the north
To make his bleak winds kiss my parched lips
And comfort me with cold. I do not ask you much;
I beg cold comfort; and you are so strait
And so ingrateful you deny me that. [V.vii]
King John to Prince Henry asking for something for the
pain from the poison

This England never did, nor never shall,
Lie at the proud foot of a conqueror,
But when it first did help to wound itself.
Now these her princes are come home again,
Come the three corners of the world in arms,
And we shall shock them. Nought shall make
us rue,
If England to itself do rest but true. [V.vii]
Philip the Bastard to Prince Henry on the renewed
invincibility of England

Richard II

Written 1595
Time and place of action 14th-Century England

Richard II's hold on the English throne is precarious. The people are becoming increasingly discontent with the King's extravagant lifestyle and the heavy taxation imposed on them. Richard's uncle, John of Gaunt, is one of the only steadying influences and continually warns Richard of the consequences of bad government. Richard, confident in the belief of the divine protection of kings, ignores his advice. When John of Gaunt dies Richard confiscates his land and wealth instead of passing it on to the exiled Henry Bolingbroke, John's son. Bolingbroke leads a rebellion against Richard who is forced to renounce the throne and confess publicly his crimes. Richard is imprisoned and murdered. Although Bolingbroke did not actually order the murder, it was done on his wishes. He decides to make a pilgrimage to the Holy Land to atone for this crime

Let's purge this choler without letting blood. [I.i]
*Richard attempts to end the quarrel between Henry
Bolingbroke and the Duke of Norfolk*

The language I have learnt these forty years,
My native English, now I must forego;
And now my tongue's use is to me no more
Than an unstringed viol or a harp. [I.iii]
Duke of Norfolk, on being banished by Richard

But what thou art, God, thou, and I, do know;
And all too soon, I fear, the king shall rue.
[I.iii]
*The Duke of Norfolk to Bolingbroke, saying that the King
will regret his action*

How long a time lies in one little word!
Four lagging winters and four wanton springs
End in a word: such is the breath of kings. [I.iii]
*Bolingbroke on having his banishment reduced from ten
to six years' length*

Must I not serve a long apprenticehood
To foreign passages; and in the end,
Having my freedom, boast of nothing else
But that I was a journeyman to grief? [I.iii]
Bolingbroke on being exiled

All places that the eye of heaven visits
Are to a wise man ports and happy havens.
Teach thy necessity to reason thus:
There is no virtue like necessity.
Think not the King did banish thee,
But thou the King. [I.iii]
John of Gaunt comforting Bolingbroke on being exiled

Then, England's ground, farewell; sweet soil, adieu;
My mother, and my nurse, that bears me yet!
Where'er I wander, boast of this I can:
Though banish'd, yet a trueborn English man. [I.iii]
Bolingbroke on being exiled

Methinks I am a prophet new inspir'd,
And thus expiring do foretell of him:
His rash fierce blaze of riot cannot last,
For violent fires soon burn out themselves;
Small showers last long, but sudden storms are short;
He tires betimes that spurs too fast betimes;
With eager feeding food doth choke the feeder;
Light vanity, insatiate cormorant,
Consuming means, soon preys upon itself.
This royal throne of kings, this scept'red isle,
This earth of majesty, this seat of Mars,
This other Eden, demi-paradise,
This fortress built by Nature for herself

Against infection and the hand of war,
This happy breed of men, this little world,
This precious stone set in the silver sea,
Which serves it in the office of a wall,
Or as a moat defensive to a house,
Against the envy of less happier lands;
This blessed plot, this earth, this realm, this
England,
This nurse, this teeming womb of royal kings,
Fear'd by their breed, and famous by their birth,
Renowned for their deeds as far from home,
For Christian service and true chivalry,
As is the sepulchre in stubborn Jewry
Of the world's ransom, blessed Mary's Son;
This land of such dear souls, this dear dear land,
Dear for her reputation through the world,
Is now leas'd out, I die pronouncing it,
Like to a tenement or pelting farm.
England, bound in with the triumphant sea,
Whose rocky shore beats back the envious siege
Of wat'ry Neptune, is now bound in with shame,
With inky blots and rotten parchment bonds;
That England, that was wont to conquer others,
Hath made a shameful conquest of itself.
[II.i]
John of Gaunt is dying, and expresses his fears for his beloved England

Thy death-bed is no lessser than thy land
Wherein thou liest in reputation sick;
And thou, too careless patient as thou art,
Commit'st thy anointed body to the cure
Of those physicians that first wounded thee:
A thousand flatterers sit within thy crown,
Whose compass is no bigger than thy head;
And yet, incaged in so small a verge,
The waste is no whit lesser than thy land. [II.i]
*John of Gaunt, dying, warns Richard of bad government
and listening to flatterers*

Not all the water in the rough rude sea
Can wash the balm off from an anointed king;
The breath of worldly men cannot depose
The deputy elected by the Lord.
For every man that Bolingbroke hath press'd
To lift shrewd steel against our golden crown,
God for his Richard hath in heavenly pay
A glorious angel. Then, if angels fight,
Weak men must fall; for heaven still guards the
right. [III.ii]
*Richard, convinced of the divine protection of kings, is
not afraid of Bolingbroke's attack*

O villains, vipers, damn'd without redemption!
Dogs, easily won to fawn on any man!

Snakes, in my heart-blood warm'd, that sting my
heart!
Three Judases, each one thrice worse than Judas!
Would they make peace? Terrible hell make war
Upon their spotted souls for this offence!
[III.ii]
*Richard curses his so-called friends for turning their
allegiance to Bolingbroke*

For God's sake let us sit upon the ground
And tell sad stories of the death of kings:
How some have been depos'd, some slain in war,
Some haunted by the ghosts they have depos'd,
Some poison'd by their wives, some sleeping kill'd,
All murder'd: for within the hollow crown
That rounds the mortal temples of a king
Keeps Death his court; and there the antic sits,
Scoffing his state and grinning at his pomp;
Allowing him a breath, a little scene,
To monarchize, be fear'd, and kill with looks;
Infusing him with self and vain conceit,
As if this flesh which walls about our life
Were brass impregnable; and, humour'd thus,
Comes at the last, and with a little pin
Bores through his castle wall, and farewell king!
[III.ii]
*Richard has realised that he is not protected by divine
power. He mourns the death of kings*

What must the King do now? Must he submit?
The king shall do it. Must he be depos'd?
The king shall be contented. Must he lose
The name of king? A God's name, let it go.
I'll give my jewels for a set of beads,
My gorgeous palace for a hermitage,
My gay apparel for an almsman's gown,
My figur'd goblets for a dish of wood,
My sceptre for a palmer's walking staff,
My subjects for a pair of carved saints,
And my large kingdom for a little grave,
A little little grave, an obscure grave;
Or I'll be buried in the king's high way,
Some way of common trade, where subjects' feet
May hourly trample on their sovereign's head;
For on my heart they tread now whilst I live,
And buried once, why not upon my head? [III.iii]
Richard is disconsolate at losing his kingdom

Why should we, in the compass of a pale,
Keep law and form and due proportion,
Showing, as in a model, our firm estate,
When our sea-walled garden, the whole land,
Is full of weeds; her fairest flowers chok'd up,
Her fruit trees all unprun'd, her hedges ruin'd,
Her knots disordered, and her wholesome herbs
Swarming with caterpillars? [III.iv]
The servant, using an overgrown garden as an allegory

for England under Richard's rule, wants to know why
they should bother with law and order

And if you crown him, let me prophesy –
The blood of English shall manure the ground,
And future ages groan for this foul act;
Peace shall go sleep with Turks and infidels,
And in this seat of peace tumultuous wars
Shall kin with kin and kind with kind confound;
Disorder, horror, fear, and mutiny,
Shall here inhabit, and this land be call'd
The field of Golgotha and dead men's skulls. [IV.i]
The Bishop of Carlisle speaks against the crowning of
Bolingbroke as king and prophesies civil war if Richard is
deposed

Mine eyes are full of tears; I cannot see.
And yet salt water blinds them not so much
But they can see a sort of traitors here.
Nay, if I turn mine eyes upon myself,
I find myself a traitor with the rest;
For I have given here my soul's consent
T' undeck the pompous body of a king;
Made glory base, and sovereignty a slave,
Proud majesty a subject, state a peasant. [IV.i]
Richard theatrically apportioning some of the blame for
losing the crown to himself

A brittle glory shineth in this face;
As brittle as the glory is the face. [IV.i]
Richard dashes a mirror against the floor

In winter's tedious nights sit by the fire
With good old folks, and let them tell thee tales
Of woeful ages long ago betid;
And ere thou bid good night, to quit their griefs,
Tell thou the lamentable tale of me,
And send the hearers weeping to their beds. [V.i]
Richard bidding farewell to his wife for the last time

As in a theatre the eyes of men
After a well-grac'd actor leaves the stage
Are idly bent on him that enters next,
Thinking his prattle to be tedious;
Even so, or with much more contempt, men's eyes
Did scowl on gentle Richard. [V.ii]
The Duke of York recounting Richard's departure in procession after Bolingbroke

I have been studying how I may compare
This prison where I live unto the world. [V.v]
Richard in the dungeon of Pomfret Castle

I wasted time, and now doth time waste me. [V.v]
Richard in the dungeon musing over his wasted life

Mount, mount, my soul! thy seat is up on high;
Whilst my gross flesh sinks downward here to die.
[V.v]
Richard, having defending himself gallantly, is murdered

They love not poison that do poison need,
Nor do I thee. Though I did wish him dead,
I hate the murderer, love him murdered. [V.vi]
*Bolingbroke, on being presented with Richard's dead
body. Although he did not actually order the murder, he
intimated that was what he wanted*

Henry IV, Part 1

Written 1596-7
Time and place of action Early 15th-Century
   England

*Henry IV is uneasy over his part in the deposition
and murder of Richard II. He is also worried
about his wayward son, Prince Hal, who consorts
with John Falstaff. His planned trip to the Holy
Land has to be postponed because of rebellions in
Scotland and Wales. The Scottish rebellion is*

quelled by Hotspur. King Henry compares his son unfavourably to the valiant Hotspur. However, Hotspur becomes disillusioned with the King whom he believes does not show him enough gratitude for his help in deposing King Richard. The King believes Hotspur is becoming too proud. Hotspur decides to join the Scottish and Welsh in fighting the King. Prince Hal, casting aside his wayward life-style, pledges his help to the King and valiantly kills Hotspur in battle. Henry is safe to continue his reign.

So shaken as we are, so wan with care,
Find we a time for frighted peace to pant
And breathe short-winded accents of new broils
To be commenc'd in strands afar remote. [I.i]
King Henry is enjoying an uneasy peace a year after the death of King Richard

In those holy fields
Over whose acres walk'd those blessed feet
Which fourteen hundred years ago were nail'd
For our advantage on the bitter cross. [I.i]
Henry is planning his trip to the Holy Land to atone for his part in the murder of King Richard

Unless hours were cups of sack, and minutes
capons, and clocks the tongues of bawds, and dials

the signs of leaping-houses, and the blessed sun
himself a fair hot wench in flame-coloured taffeta, I
see no reason why thou shouldst be so superfluous
to demand the time of day. [I.ii]
Prince Hal to his great friend, Falstaff

Shall there be gallows standing in England when
thou art king, and resolution thus fubb'd as it is
with the rusty curb of old father antic, the law? [I.ii]
Falstaff to Prince Hal

I know you all, and will awhile uphold
The unyok'd humour of your idleness;
Yet herein will I imitate the sun,
Who doth permit the base contagious clouds
To smother up his beauty from the world,
That, when he please again to be himself,
Being wanted, he may be more wond'red at
By breaking through the foul and ugly mists
Of vapours that did seem to strangle him.
If all the year were playing holidays,
To sport would be as tedious as to work;
But when they seldom come, they wish'd for come,
And nothing pleaseth but rare accidents.
So, when this loose behaviour I throw off
And pay the debt I never promised,
By how much better than my word I am,
By so much shall I falsify men's hopes;

And, like bright metal on a sullen ground,
My reformation, glitt'ring o'er my fault,
Shall show more goodly and attract more eyes
Than that which hath no foil to set it off.
I'll so offend to make offence a skill,
Redeeming time when men think least I will. [I.ii]
*Prince Hal soliloquises on the time when he will cast
aside his wayward existence and take up the mantle of
king. It shows his astuteness and foretells the time when
Falstaff will lose favour*

And as the soldiers bore dead bodies by,
He call'd them untaught knaves, unmannerly,
To bring a slovenly unhandsome corse
Betwixt the wind and his nobility.
With many holiday and lady terms
He questioned me. [I.iii]
*Hotspur talking disdainfully of the King's messenger
who came to him on the battlefield*

To put down Richard, that sweet lovely rose,
And plant this thorn, this canker, Bolingbroke? [I.iii]
*Hotspur regretting his part in the overthrow of King
Richard*

By heaven, methinks it were an easy leap
To pluck bright honour from the pale-fac'd moon;
Or dive into the bottom of the deep,

Where fathom-line could never touch the ground,
And pluck up drowned honour by the locks. [I.iii]
Hotspur, looking for glory, plans to join forces with the
rebel Scottish and Welsh against King Henry

Falstaff sweats to death
And lards the lean earth as he walks along. [II.ii]
Hal describes Falstaff who's lost his horse and has to walk

Constant you are,
But yet a woman; and for secrecy,
No lady closer; for I well believe
Thou wilt not utter what thou dost not know. [II.iii]
Hotspur is not prepared to reveal his plot to his wife
because she is a woman

He that kills me some six or seven dozen of Scots at
a breakfast, washes his hands and says to his wife
'Fie upon this quiet life! I want work'. [II.iv]
Prince Hal mocking Hotspur's energetic valour

Nay, that's past praying for: I have pepper'd two of
them; two I am sure I have paid – two rogues in
buckram suits. I tell thee what, Hal, if I tell thee a
lie, spit in my face, call me horse. Thou knowest my
old ward: here I lay, and thus I bore my point. Four
rogues in buckram let drive at me. [II.iv]
Falstaff recounting his ambush to the Prince is exagger-
ating dreadfully

A plague of sighing and grief! it blows a man up
like a bladder. [II.iv]
Falstaff blames his hard life for his huge proportions

No, my good lord: banish Peto, banish Bardolph,
banish Poins; but, for sweet Jack Falstaff, kind Jack
Falstaff, true Jack Falstaff, valiant Jack Falstaff – and
therefore more valiant, being, as he is, old Jack
Falstaff – banish not him thy Harry's company, banish not him thy Harry's company. Banish plump
Jack, and banish all the world. [II.iv]
*Falstaff, pretending to be Prince Hal defending Falstaff to
his father, the King*

Glendower: At my nativity
The front of heaven was full of fiery shapes,
Of burning cressets; and at my birth
The frame and huge foundation of the earth
Shaked like a coward.
Hotspur: Why, so it would have done at the same
season if your mother's cat had but kittened. [III.i]
Glendower boasting of his supernatural powers

And all the courses of my life do show
I am not in the roll of common men. [III.i]
Glendower talking of himself

Glendower: I can call spirits from the vasty deep.

221

Hotspur: Why, so can I, or so can any man;
But will they come when you do call for them? [III.i]
Hotspur is highly sceptical of Glendower's claims

I'll have the current in this place damm'd up,
And here the smug and silver Trent shall run
In a new channel, fair and evenly. [III.i]
*Hotspur is not happy with the proposed division of
England and his share of it*

I had rather be a kitten and cry mew
Than one of these same metre ballad-mongers.
[III.i]
Hotspur does not enjoy music and poetry

O, he is as tedious
As a tired horse, a railing wife;
Worse than a smoky house; I had rather live
With cheese and garlic in a windmill, far,
Than feed on cates and have him talk to me
In any summer house in Christendom. [III.i]
*Hotspur telling Mortimer how much he dislikes
Glendower*

The skipping King, he ambled up and down
With shallow jesters and rash bavin wits.
[III.ii]
King Henry referring to King Richard and his entourage

Being daily swallowed by men's eyes,
They surfeited with honey and began
To loathe the taste of sweetness, whereof a little
More than a little is by much too much.
So, when he had occasion to be seen,
He was but as the cuckoo is in June,
Heard, not regarded. [III.ii]
King Henry recounts how the people became fed up with
King Richard. He is afraid Prince Hal might be the same

My nearest and dearest enemy? [III.ii]
King Henry referring to Prince Hal

I will redeem all this on Percy's head,
And in the closing of some glorious day
Be bold to tell you that I am your son. [III.ii]
Prince Hal telling King Henry of the day when he will
kill Hotspur and redeem his reputation

Company, villainous company, hath been the spoil
of me. [III.iii]
Falstaff to Bardolph

Thou knowest in the state of innocency Adam fell;
and what should poor Jack Falstaff do in the days of
villainy? Thou seest I have more flesh than another
man, and therefore more frailty. [III.iii]
Falstaff to Prince Hal trying to justify himself

Where is his son,
The nimble-footed madcap Prince of Wales,
And his comrades that daff'd the world aside
And bid it pass? [IV.i]
*Hotspur asking where Price Hal is. The King has sent his
army against the rebels*

I saw young Harry with his beaver on,
His cushes on his thighs, gallantly arm'd,
Rise from the ground like feathered Mercury,
And vaulted with such ease into his seat
As if an angel dropp'd down from the clouds
To turn and wind a fiery Pegasus,
And witch the world with noble horsemanship. [IV.i]
Vernon to Hotspur, indicating the change in Prince Hal

For mine own part, I could be well content
To entertain the lag-end of my life
With quiet hours. [V.i]
Worcester, one of the rebels, to King Henry

I do not think a braver gentleman,
More active-valiant or more valiant-young,
More daring or more bold, is now alive
To grace this latter age with noble deeds.
For my part, I may speak it to my shame,
I have a truant been to chivalry. [V.i]
Prince Hal referring to Hotspur

Honour pricks me on. Yea, but how if honour prick
me off when I come on? How then? Can honour set
to a leg? No. Or an arm? No. Or take away the grief
of a wound? No. Honour hath no skill in surgery,
then? No. What is honour? A word. What is in that
word? Honour. What is that honour? Air. A trim
reckoning! Who hath it? He that died o'
Wednesday. Doth he feel it? No. Doth he hear it?
No. 'Tis insensible, then? Yea, to the dead. But will
it not live with the living? No. Why? Detraction will
not suffer it. Therefore I'll none of it. Honour is a
mere scutcheon. And so ends my catechism. [V.i]
*Falstaff debating between whether he would rather have
honour or death*

O, Harry, thou hast robb'd me of my youth!
I better brook the loss of brittle life
Than those proud titles thou hast won of me:
They wound my thoughts worse than thy sword
my flesh. [V.iv]
Hotspur to Prince Hal on being killed by him

Fare thee well, great heart!
Ill-weav'd ambition, how much art thou shrunk!
When that this body did contain a spirit,
A kingdom for it was too small a bound;
But now two paces of the vilest earth
Is room enough. This earth that bears thee dead

Bears not alive so stout a gentleman. [V.iv]
Prince Hal to Hotspur on killing him

What, old acquaintance! could not all this flesh
Keep in a little life? Poor Jack, farewell!
I could have better spar'd a better man. [V.iv]
*Prince Hal coming across the apparently lifeless body of
Falstaff*

The better part of valour is discretion; in the which
better part I have saved my life. [V.iv]
Falstaff pretended to be dead for his own protection

Lord, Lord, how this world is given to lying! I grant
you I was down and out of breath, and so was he;
but we rose both at an instant, and fought a long
hour by Shrewsbury clock. [V.iv]
*Falstaff pretending to Prince Hal that he had killed
Hotspur*

For my part, if a lie may do thee grace,
I'll gild it with the happiest terms I have. [V.iv]
*Prince Hal is prepared to accept Falstaff's outrageous
claims*

I'll purge, and leave sack, and live cleanly, as a
nobleman should do. [V.iv]
Falstaff promises to reform

Henry IV, Part 2

Written 1697-8
Time and place of action Early 15th-Century
England

Despite the victory over Hotspur the rebellions continue against Henry IV. The Archbishop of York has joined the rebellion claiming to avenge the murder of Richard II. Prince Hal continues to frequent the company of Falstaff and Henry is afraid he has a son who will never be fit to rule. The King's forces defeat the rebels and he becomes gravely ill. Prince Hal assures his dying father that he will cast aside his wayward lifestyle and accept the responsibilities of king. He is crowned Henry V and the play closes with him casting aside Falstaff.

I speak of peace while covert enmity,
Under the smile of safety, wounds the world.
[Induction]
King Henry has defeated Hotspur and the rebellion but there is still disquiet

Rumour is a pipe
Blown by surmises, jealousies, conjectures,
And of so easy and so plain a stop
That the blunt monster with uncounted heads,
The still-discordant wav'ring multitude,
Can play upon it. [Induction]
Rumours abound

Yet the first bringer of unwelcome news
Hath but a losing office, and his tongue
Sounds ever after as a sullen bell,
Rememb'red tolling a departing friend. [I.i]
*Northumberland on Morton bringing news of Hotspur's
death to his father*

But now the Bishop
Turns insurrection to religion.
Suppos'd sincere and holy in his thoughts,
He's follow'd both with body and with mind;
And doth enlarge his rising with the blood
Of fair King Richard. [I.i]
*The Archbishop of York has joined the rebellion, deter-
mined to avenge the murder of King Richard*

The brain of this foolish-compounded clay, man, is
not able to invent anything that intends to laughter,
more than I invent or is invented on me. I am not
only witty in myself, but the cause that wit is in

other men. I do here walk before thee like a sow
that hath overwhelm'd all her litter but one. [I.ii]
Falstaff boasting about himself to his page

Have you not a moist eye, a dry hand, a yellow
cheek, a white beard, a decreasing leg, an increasing
belly? Is not your voice broken, your wind short,
your chin double, your wit single, and every part
about you blasted with antiquity? And will you yet
call yourself young? Fie, fie, fie, Sir John! [I.ii]
*The Chief Justice pointing out to Falstaff that he is an old
man*

Chief Justice: God send the Prince a better companion!
Falstaff: God send the companion a better prince! I
cannot rid my hands of him. [I.ii]
Falstaff implying how much Prince Hal needs him

I can get no remedy against this consumption of the
purse; borrowing only lingers and lingers it out, but
the disease is incurable. [I.ii]
Falstaff is a spendthrift

When we mean to build,
We first survey the plot, then draw the model;
And when we see the figure of the house,
Then must we rate the cost of the erection;
Which if we find outweighs ability,

What do we then but draw anew the model
In fewer offices, or at least desist
To build at all? [I.iii]
Lord Bardolph discussing whether they have the means to take on the King and his armies

A hundred mark is a long one for a poor lone woman to bear; and I have borne, and borne, and borne; and have been fubb'd off, and fubb'd off, and fubb'd off, from this day to that day, that it is a shame to be thought on. [II.i]
Mistress Quickly complaining that Falstaff has not paid her back the money she lent him

He hath eaten me out of house and home. [II.i]
Mistress Quickly talking of Falstaff

Doth it not show vilely in me to desire small beer? [II.ii]
Prince Hal on his continued frequenting of the Eastcheap tavern

Is it not strange that desire should so many years outlive performance? [II.iv]
Poins to Prince Hal commenting on Falstaff's wooing of a young tart

O sleep, O gentle sleep,
Nature's soft nurse, how have I frighted thee,
That thou no more wilt weigh my eyelids down,
And steep my senses in forgetfulness?
Why rather, sleep, liest thou in smoky cribs,
Upon uneasy pallets stretching thee,
And hush'd with buzzing night-flies to thy slumber,
Than in the perfum'd chambers of the great,
Under the canopies of costly state,
And lull'd with sound of sweetest melody? [III.i]
The King, worried about the state of his kingdom, cannot sleep

Uneasy lies the head that wears a crown. [III.i]
The King talking of his own situation

O God! that one might read the book of fate,
And see the revolution of the times
Make mountains level, and the continent,
Weary of solid firmness, melt itself
Into the sea. [III.i]
King Henry would like to know what the future holds

There is a history in all men's lives,
Figuring the natures of the times deceas'd;
The which observ'd, a man may prophesy,
With a near aim, of the main chance of things

As yet not come to life, which in their seeds
And weak beginning lie intreasured. [III.i]
*Warwick to the King, saying that by studying the past
you can get a good idea of how the future will turn out*

We have heard the chimes at midnight, Master
Shallow. [III.ii]
Falstaff remembering old days of carousing

A man cannot make him laugh – but that's no marvel; he drinks no wine. [IV.iii]
*Falstaff describing the sober, young Prince John – so
unlike Prince Hal*

The Prince will, in the perfectness of time,
Cast off his followers; and their memory
Shall be as a pattern or a measure live
By which his Grace must mete the lives of other,
Turning past evils to advantages. [IV.iv]
*Warwick reassuring the dying King that Prince Hal will
turn from his wayward life and reject bad company using
what he has learnt to his own advantage*

O polish'd perturbation! golden care!
That keep'st the ports of slumber open wide
To many a watchful night! Sleep with it now!
Yet not so sound and half so deeply sweet
As he whose brow with homely biggin bound

Snores out the watch of night. [IV.v]
Prince Hal sees the crown on the pillow by his sleeping
father

God knows, my son,
By what by-paths and indirect crook'd ways
I met this crown; and I myself know well
How troublesome it sat upon my head:
To thee it shall descend with better quiet,
Better opinion, better confirmation;
For all the soil of the achievement goes
With me into the earth. [IV.v]
The dying King to his son, Prince Hal, stating that his
own rule should be more peaceful and that the hatred
incurred for King Richard's death will go with him into
the grave, hopefully wiping the slate clean

The tide of blood in me
Hath proudly flow'd in vanity till now.
Now doth it turn and ebb back to the sea,
Where it shall mingle with the state of floods,
And flow henceforth in formal majesty.
Now call we our high court of parliament;
And let us choose such limbs of noble counsel,
That the great body of our state may go
In equal rank with the best govern'd nation. [V.ii]
Prince Hal, now King Henry V, seeks to amend his ways
and surround himself with wise counsel

Let us take any man's horses: the laws of England
are at my commandment. [V.iii]
*Falstaff believes being such a good friend of the new King
will make him one of the most powerful men in England*

I know thee not, old man. Fall to thy prayers.
How ill white hairs become a fool and jester!
I have long dreamt of such a kind of man,
So surfeit-swell'd, so old, and so profane. [V.v]
*Prince Hal, now King Henry V, treats Falstaff as a
stranger*

Make less thy body hence, and more thy grace;
Leave gormandising; know the grave doth gape
For thee thrice wider than for other men –
Reply not to me with a fool-born jest;
Presume not that I am the thing I was,
For God doth know, so shall the world perceive,
That I have turn'd away my former self;
So will I those that kept me company. [V.v]
*Prince Hal, now King Henry V, will see Falstaff again if
he is willing to reform*

I will lay odds that, ere this year expire,
We bear our civil swords and native fire
As far as France. [V.v]
Prince John forsees war with France

Henry V

Written 1697-8
Time and place of action Early 15th-Century
England and France

*Prince Hal has become a wise and good ruler.
Persuaded that he has a legitimate right to the
French throne, he plans a campaign against
France. Despite being completely outnumbered, he
rallies the English soldiers and they enjoy a glori-
ous victory at Agincourt. An alliance between
France and England is forged with the marriage of
King Henry V with Katherine of France.*

Can this cockpit hold
The vasty fields of France? or may we cram
Within this wooden O the very casques
That did affright the air at Agincourt? [I, Prologue]
*Given the limitations of the theatre and the great battle to
be re-enacted, the Chorus asks the audience to use their
imagination*

The breath no sooner left his father's body
But that his wildness, mortified in him,
Seem'd to die too; yea, at that very moment,
Consideration like an angel came
And whipp'd th' offending Adam out of him. [I.i]
The Archbishop of Canterbury and the Bishop of Ely discuss how Prince Hal has matured into a good king

You are their heir; you sit upon their throne. [I.ii]
The Bishop of Ely telling King Henry he has a rightful claim to the French throne

For so work the honey-bees,
Creatures that by a rule in nature teach
The act of order to a peopled kingdom.
They have a king, and officers of sorts,
Where some like magistrates correct at home;
Others like merchants venture trade abroad;
Others like soldiers, armed in their stings,
Make boot upon the summer's velvet buds,
Which pillage they with merry march bring home
To the tent-royal of their emperor;
Who, busied in his majesty, surveys
The singing masons building roofs of gold,
The civil citizens kneading up the honey,
The poor mechanic porters crowding in
Their heavy burdens at his narrow gate,
The sad-ey'd justice, with his surly hum,

Delivering o'er to executors pale
The lazy yawning drone. [I.ii]
*The Archbishop likens England to a community of bees
with each member carrying out their specific task*

King Henry: What treasure, uncle?
Exeter: Tennis-balls, my liege. [I.ii]
The gift from the French Dauphin is an intended insult

His present and your pains we thank you for.
When we have match'd our rackets to these balls,
We will in France, by God's grace, play a set
Shall strike his father's crown into the hazard. [I.ii]
*King Henry is angry and is prepared to avenge this
insult on French soil*

Now all the youth of England are on fire,
And silken dalliance in the wardrobe lies;
Now thrive the armourers, and honour's thought
Reigns solely in the breast of every man;
They sell the pasture now to buy the horse,
Following the mirror of all Christian kings
With winged heels, as English Mercuries.
For now sits Expectation in the air,
And hides a sword from hilts unto the point
With crowns imperial, crowns, and coronets,
Promis'd to Harry and his followers. [II, Prologue]
*The youth of England are excited at the prospect of
fighting France*

He's in Arthur's bosom, if ever man went to
Arthur's bosom. 'A made a finer end, and went
away an it had been any christom child; 'a parted
ev'n just between twelve and one, ev'n at th' turning o' the tide; for after I saw him fumble with the
sheets, and play with flowers, and smile upon his
fingers' end, I knew there was but one way; for his
nose was as sharp as a pen, and 'a babbl'd of green
fields.'How now, Sir John!' quoth I 'What, man, be
o' good cheer.' So 'a cried out 'God, God, God!'
three or four times. Now I, to comfort him, bid him
'a should not think of God; I hop'd there was no
need to trouble himself with any such thoughts yet.
So 'a bade me lay more clothes on his feet; I put my
hand into the bed and felt them, and they were as
cold as any stone; then I felt to his knees, and so
upward and upward, and all was as cold as any
stone. [II.iii]
Mistress Quickly describes Falstaff's death

Once more unto the breach, dear friends, once
more;
Or close the wall up with our English dead.
In peace there's nothing so becomes a man
As modest stillness and humility;
But when the blast of war blows in our ears,
Then imitate the action of the tiger:
Stiffen the sinews, summon up the blood,

Disguise fair nature with hard-favour'd rage;
Then lend the eye a terrible aspect. [III.i]
The English King rallying his men in France

And you, good yeomen,
Whose limbs were made in England, show us here
The mettle of your pasture. [III.i]
King Henry rallying his men against the French

I see you stand like greyhounds in the slips,
Straining upon the start. The game's afoot:
Follow your spirit; and, upon this charge
Cry 'God for Harry, England, and Saint George!'
[III.i]
King Henry rallying his men against the French

That island of England breeds very valiant crea-
tures; their mastiffs are of unmatchable courage.
[III.vii]
*Rambures discussing the English with the French
Dauphin*

Now entertain conjecture of a time
When creeping murmur and the poring dark
Fills the wide vessel of the universe.
From camp to camp, through the foul womb of night,
The hum of either army stilly sounds,
That the fix'd sentinels almost receive

The secret whispers of each other's watch.
Fire answers fire, and through their paly flames
Each battle sees the other's umber'd face;
Steed threatens steed, in high and boastful neighs
Piercing the night's dull ear; and from the tents
The armourers accomplishing the knights,
With busy hammers closing rivets up,
Give dreadful note of preparation. [IV, Prologue]
The French and English armies wait for dawn

Gloucester, 'tis true that we are in great danger;
The greater therefore should our courage be. [IV.i]
*King Henry is undaunted by the odds against the
English*

He may show what outward courage he will; but I
believe, as cold a night as 'tis, he could wish himself
in Thames up to the neck; and so I would he were,
and I by him, at all adventures, so we were quit
here. [IV.i]
*Bates, a soldier, to the disguised King. The soldiers think
the King is as afraid as they.*

But if the cause be not good, the King himself hath a
heavy reckoning to make when all those legs and
arms and heads, chopp'd off in a battle, shall join
together at the latter day and cry all 'We died at
such a place' – some swearing, some crying for a

surgeon, some upon their wives left poor behind them, some upon the debts they owe, some upon their children rawly left. I am afeard there are few die well that die in a battle; for how can they charitably dispose of anything when blood is their argument? Now, if these men do not die well, it will be a black matter for the king that led them to it; who to disobey were against all proportion of subjection. [IV.i]

Williams speaks for all the common soldiers who have died for the quarrels of kings and not their own

'Tis not the balm, the sceptre, and the ball,
The sword, the mace, the crown imperial,
The intertissued robe of gold and pearl,
The farced title running fore the king,
The throne he sits on, nor the tide of pomp
That beats upon the high shore of this world –
No, not all these, thrice gorgeous ceremony,
Not all these, laid in bed majestical,
Can sleep so soundly as the wretched slave,
Who, with a body fill'd and vacant mind,
Gets him to rest, cramm'd with distressful bread;
Never sees horrid night, the child of hell;
But, like a lackey, from the rise to set
Sweats in the eye of Phoebus, and all night
Sleeps in Elycium. [IV.i]

King Henry on the great responsibility of a ruler

O God of battles, steel my soldiers' hearts,
Possess them not with fear! Take from them now
The sense of reck'ning, if th' opposed numbers
Pluck their hearts from them! Not to-day, O Lord,
O, not to-day, think not upon the fault
My father made in compassing the crown. [IV.i]
*King Henry prays for his men and asks God not to
remember the crime committed by his father in deposing
King Richard*

If we are mark'd to die, we are enow
To do our country loss; and if to live,
The fewer men, the greater share of honour. [IV.iii]
*King Henry tells his men that if they are successful the
honour will be even greater*

He which hath no stomach to this fight,
Let him depart; his passport shall be made,
And crowns for convoy put into his purse;
We would not die in that man's company
That fears his fellowship to die with us.
This day is call'd the feast of Crispian.
He that outlives this day, and comes safe home,
Will stand a tip-toe when this day is nam'd,
And rouse him at the name of Crispian.
He that shall live this day, and see old age,
Will yearly on the vigil feast his neighbours,
And say 'To-morrow is Saint Crispian'.

Then he will strip his sleeve and show his scars,
And say 'These wounds I had on Crispian's day'.
Old men forget; yet all shall be forgot,
But he'll remember, with advantages,
What feats he did that day. Then shall our names,
Familiar in his mouth as household words –
Harry the King, Bedford and Exeter,
Warwick and Talbot, Salisbury and Gloucester –
Be in their flowing cups freshly rememb'red.
This story shall the good man teach his son;
And Crispin Crispian shall ne'er go by,
From this day to the ending of the world,
But we in it shall be remembered –
We few, we happy few, we band of brothers;
For he to-day that sheds his blood with me
Shall be my brother; be he ne'er so vile,
This day shall gentle his condition;
And gentlemen in England now a-bed
Shall think themselves accurs'd they were not here,
And hold their manhoods cheap whiles any speaks
That fought with us upon Saint Crispin's day. [IV.iii]
King Henry rallies his men before the Battle of Agincourt

I warrant you sall find, in the comparisons between
Macedon and Monmouth, that the situations, look
you, is both alike. There is a river in Macedon; and
there is also moreover a river at Monmouth; it is cal-
l'd Wye at Monmouth, but it is out of my prains

what is the name of the other river; but 'tis all one,
'tis alike as my fingers is to my fingers, and there is
salmons in both. [IV.vii]
Fluellen's personal version of geography

Let it not disgrace me
If I demand, before this royal view,
What rub or what impediment there is
Why that the naked, poor, and mangled Peace,
Dear nurse of arts, plenties, and joyful births,
Should not in this best garden of the world,
Our fertile France, put up her lovely visage? [V.ii]
The Duke of Burgundy desiring peace with England

But, before God, Kate, I cannot look greenly, nor
gasp out my eloquence, nor I have no cunning in
protestation; only downright oaths, which I never
use till urg'd, nor never break for urging. If thou
canst love a fellow of this temper, Kate, whose face
is not worth sun-burning, that never looks in his
glass for love of anything he sees there, let thine eye
be thy cook. [V.ii]
*King Henry knows he is not an eloquent lover, but asks
Katherine to accept him*

It is not a fashion for the maids in France to kiss
before they are married, would she say?…
O Kate, nice customs curtsy to great kings. [V.ii]
King Henry overrides French customs

Combine your hearts in one, your realms in one!
As man and wife, being two, are one in love,
So be there 'twixt your kingdoms such a spousal
That never may ill office or fell jealousy,
Which troubles oft the bed of blessed marriage,
Thrust in between the paction of these kingdoms. [V.ii]
Queen Isabel hoping the marriage of Henry and Katherine
will mirror the marriage of France and England

Henry VI, Part 1

Written Before 1592
Time and place of action Early 15th-Century
England and France

Henry V has just died, leaving his young son to
become King Henry VI. There is growing unrest in
France over the English possessions. A quarrel
between the houses of Lancaster and York heralds
the Wars of the Roses. Henry VI is a weak king
and the Duke of Suffolk gains power over him by
arranging Henry's marriage with Margaret,
Suffolk's lover. In France Joan of Arc is leading
the French to victory over the English.

Hung be the heavens with black, yield day to night!
Comets, importing change of times and states,
Brandish your crystal tresses in the sky
And with them scourge the bad revolting stars
That have consented unto Henry's death! [I.i]
England is mourning King Henry, the famous victor at
Agincourt

Orleans is besiege'd;
The English army is grown weak and faint;
The Earl of Salisbury craveth supply
And hardly keeps his men from mutiny. [I.i]
The English interests in France are being taken back by
the French

Assign'd am I to be the English scourge.
This night the siege assuredly I'll raise.
Expect Saint Martin's summer, halcyon days,
Since I have entered into these wars.
Glory is like a circle in the water,
Which never ceaseth to enlarge itself
Till by broad spreading it disperse itself to nought.
With Henry's death the English circle ends;
Dispersed are the glories it included. [I.ii]
Joan of Arc raising French morale

'Tis Joan, not we, by whom the day is won;
For which I will divide my crown with her;

And all the priests and friars in my realm
Shall in procession sing her endless praise. [I.vi]
*Charles, the Dauphin, praising Joan of Arc on helping
save Orleans from the English*

Plantagenet: Let him that is a true-born gentleman
And stands upon the honour of his birth,
If he suppose that I have pleaded truth,
From off this brier pluck a white rose with me.
Somerset: Let him that is no coward nor no flatterer,
But dare maintain the party of the truth,
Pluck a red rose from off this thorn with me. [II.iv]
The beginning of the Wars of the Roses

Damsel of France, I think I have you fast.
Unchain your spirits now with spelling charms,
And try if they can gain your liberty. [V.iii]
The Duke of York to the captured Joan of Arc

She's beautiful, and therefore to be woo'd;
She is a woman, therefore to be won. [V.iii]
*Suffolk talking of Margaret whom he is in love with. As
he is already married, he persuades the King to marry her*

Margaret shall now be Queen, and rule the King;
But I will rule both her, the King, and realm.
[V.v]
Suffolk's plot to control power

Henry VI, Part 2

Written Before 1591
Time and place of action Mid 15th-Century
England

*Incensed by the loss of territories in France, the
Duke of York intends to have himself made king
instead of the weak and naive Henry VI. The King
removes his uncle Gloucester from the Lord
Protectorship, and the Duke of Suffolk contrives
Gloucester's murder. Popular rebellion breaks out,
lead by Jack Cade, who claims to be Richard II's
heir. Cade is killed, and his attempt comes to
nothing, but the Wars of the Roses break out in
earnest when York returns with an army from
Ireland to seize the crown. The King loses the battle of St Albans*

Shall Henry's conquest, Bedford's vigilance,
Your deeds of war, and all our counsel die?
O peers of England, shameful is this league!
Fatal this marriage. [I.i]
*Humphrey, Duke of Gloucester, is deeply unhappy about
King Henry's marriage and the treaty with France*

Not all these lords do vex me half so much
As that proud dame, the Lord Protector's wife.
She sweeps it through the court with troops of ladies,
More like an empress than Duke Humphrey's wife.
Strangers in court do take her for the Queen.
She bears a duke's revenues on her back,
And in her heart she scorns our poverty. [I.iii]
*The Queen hates the Duke of Gloucester's wife for her
wealth and pride*

We thank you, lords. But I am not your king
Till I be crown'd, and that my sword be stain'd
With heart-blood of the house of Lancaster. [II.ii]
The Duke of York plans to become king

But be thou mild, and blush not at my shame,
Nor stir at nothing till the axe of death
Hang over thee, as sure it shortly will. [II.iv]
*The Duchess of Gloucester, publicly humiliated, predicts
her husband's downfall*

Smooth runs the water where the brook is deep,
And in his simple show he harbours treason. [III.i]
*The Duke of Suffolk warns the King against the Duke of
Gloucester*

Ah, uncle Humphrey, in thy face I see
The map of honour, truth, and loyalty!

And yet, good Humphrey, is the hour to come
That e'er I prov'd thee false or fear'd thy faith. [III.i]
King Henry is sorrowful at his uncle's arrest

Cade: There shall be in England seven halfpenny
loaves sold for a penny; the three-hoop'd pot shall
have ten hoops; and I will make it felony to drink
small beer. All the realm shall be in common, and in
Cheapside shall my palfrey go to grass. And when I
am king – as king I will be – ... there shall be no
money; all shall eat and drink on my score, and I
will apparel them all in one livery, that they may
agree like brothers and worship me their lord.
Dick: The first thing we do, let's kill all the lawyers.
[IV.ii]
*Jack Cade and Dick the Butcher have plans for England's
'reformation'*

From Ireland thus comes York to claim his right
And pluck the crown from feeble Henry's head:
Ring bells aloud, burn bonfires clear and bright,
To entertain great England's lawful king. [V.i]
The Duke of York has come to claim the throne

O, where is faith? O, where is loyalty?
If it be banish'd from the frosty head,
Where shall it find a harbour in the earth?
Wilt thou go dig a grave to find out war

And shame thine honourable age with blood? [V.i]
The King is shocked to find the Earls of Warwick and
Salisbury joined with the rebels

What are you made of? You'll nor fight nor fly.
Now is it manhood, wisdom, and defence,
To give the enemy way, and too secure us
By what we can, which can no more but fly. [V.ii]
Queen Margaret urges King Henry to flee to London

Henry VI, Part 3

Written 1590-1
Time and place of action Mid 15th-Century
   England and France

England plunges into civil war depite Henry's
attempts to make York his eventual heir. York and
his youngest son, Rutland, are killed by Lord
Clifford, allied with Queen Margaret. York's
remaining three sons cut their way to power
through a series of battles and reversals of alle-
giance, eventually stabbing Margaret's son, the
Prince of Wales, and capturing the Queen. After

251

Richard of Gloucester has despatched King Henry to the Tower of London, York's eldest son becomes Edward IV. Margaret is banished to France.

But thou prefer'st thy life before thine honour;
And seeing thou dost, I here divorce myself
Both from thy table, Henry, and thy bed,
Until that act of parliament be repeal'd
Whereby my son is disinherited. [I.i]
Queen Margaret to her husband, King Henry, on his attempt to make York his heir

Thy father slew my father; therefore, die. [I.iii]
Clifford stabbing the youthful and innocent Rutland

How couldst thou drain the life-blood of the child,
To bid the father wipe his eyes withal,
And yet be seen to bear a woman's face?
Women are soft, mild, pitiful, and flexible:
Thou stern, obdurate, flinty, rough, remorseless. [I.iv]
The Duke of York to Queen Margaret, on her taunting him with his son's murder

But thou art neither like thy sire nor dam;
But like a foul misshapen stigmatic,
Mark'd by the destinies to be avoided,
As venom toads or lizards' dreadful stings. [II.ii]
Queen Margaret to Richard

O God! methinks it were a happy life
To be no better than a homely swain;
To sit upon a hill, as I do now,
To carve out dials quaintly, point by point,
Thereby to see the minutes how they run –
How many makes the hour full complete,
How many hours brings about the day,
How many days will finish up the year,
How many years a mortal man may live. [II.v]
King Henry wishes for a peaceful life

Love forswore me in my mother's womb;
And, for I should not deal in her soft laws,
She did corrupt frail nature with some bribe
To shrink mine arm up like a wither'd shrub;
To make an envious mountain on my back,
Where sits deformity to mock my body;
To shape my legs of an unequal size;
To disproportion me in every part,
Like to a chaos, or an unlick'd bear-whelp
That carries no impression like the dam.
And am I, then, a man to be belov'd?
O monstrous fault to harbour such a thought!
Then, since this earth affords no joy to me
But to command, to check, to o'erbear such
As are of better person than myself,
I'll make my heaven to dream upon the crown. [III.ii]
*Richard, aware of his physical imperfections, has
ambitions for the crown*

I can add colours to the chameleon,
Change shapes with Protheus for advantages,
And set the murderous Machiavel to school.
Can I do this, and cannot get a crown? [III.ii]
Richard of Gloucester is skilled in hypocrisy

A little fire is quickly trodden out,
Which, being suffer'd, rivers cannot quench.
[IV.viii]
*Clarence to King Henry, advising him to stop Edward's
advance before it is too late*

How sweet a plant have you untimely cropped!
[V.v]
*Queen Margaret after her son has been stabbed by the
Duke of York's sons*

For I will buzz abroad such propehcies
That Edward shall be fearful for his life;
And then to purge his fear, I'll be thy death.
King Henry and the Prince his son are gone.
Clarence, thy turn is next, and then the rest. [V.vi]
Richard outlines his ruthless route to the throne

Richard III

Written 1592-3
Time and place of action later 15th-Century
England

Edward Plantagenet is now king, but his brother Richard of Gloucester's desire for the crown is such that he is prepared to wipe out all those of his family who stand in his way. He contrives the imprisonment and death of his elder brother, Clarence; this in turn causes the death of the ailing King. The King's sons are disposed of in the Tower. Allies of the Queen are ruthlessly removed. No sooner has Richard gained the throne than he finds the Duke of Buckingham and the Earl of Richmond raising armies against him. Tormented by the ghosts of those he has killed, Richard is defeated at Bosworth Field and Richard's accession ends the Wars of the Roses with the establishment of Henry VII as the first Tudor monarch.

Now is the winter of our discontent
Made glorious summer by this sun of York. [I.i]
Richard talking of the peace in England

Grim-visag'd war hath smooth'd his wrinkl'd front,
And now, instead of mounting barbed steeds
To fright the souls of fearful adversaries,
He capers nimbly in a lady's chamber
To the lascivious pleasing of a lute.
But I, that am not shap'd for sportive tricks,
Nor made to court an amorous looking-glass –
I, that am rudely stamp'd, and want love's majesty
To strut before a wanton ambling nymph –
I, that am curtail'd of this fair proportion,
Cheated of feature by dissembling nature,
Deform'd, unfinish'd, sent before my time
Into this breathing world scarce half made up,
And that so lamely and unfashionable
That dogs bark at me as I halt by them;
Why, I, in this weak piping time of peace,
Have no delight to pass away the time,
Unless to spy my shadow in the sun
And descent on mine own deformity.
And therefore, since I cannot prove a lover
To entertain these fair well-spoken days,
I am determined to prove a villain
And hate the idle pleasures of these days. [I.i]
Richard soliloquises on how he is not suited for the pursuits of peace, and is determined to be evil

Was ever woman in this humour woo'd?
Was ever woman in this humour won?
I'll have her; but I will not keep her long. [I.ii]
Richard has won the lady Anne despite having killed her
husband and her father

I do the wrong, and first begin to brawl.
The secret mischiefs that I set abroach
I lay unto the grievous charge of others.
Clarence, who I indeed have cast in darkness,
I do beweep to many simple gulls;
Namely, to Derby, Hastings, Buckingham;
And tell them 'tis the Queen and her allies
That stir the King against the Duke my brother.
Now they believe it, and withal whet me
To be reveng'd on Rivers, Dorset, Grey;
But then I sigh and, with a piece of Scripture,
Tell them that God bids us do good for evil.
And thus I clothe my naked villainy
With odd old ends stol'n forth of holy writ,
And seem a saint when most I play the devil. [I.iii]
Richard sets his scheming into motion

O Lord, methought what pain it was to drown,
What dreadful noise of waters in my ears,
What sights of ugly death within my eyes!
Methought I saw a thousand fearful wrecks,
A thousand men that fishes gnaw'd upon,

Wedges of gold, great anchors, heaps of pearl,
Inestimable stones, unvalued jewels,
All scatt'red in the bottom of the sea;
Some lay in dead men's skulls, and in the holes
Where eyes did once inhabit, there were crept,
As 'twere in scorn of eyes, reflecting gems,
That woo'd the slimy bottom of the deep
And mock'd the dead bones that lay scatt'red by.
[I.iv]
Clarence, imprisoned in the Tower, recalls his nightmare

Come, come, dispatch; the Duke would be at dinner
Make a short shrift; he longs to see your head. [III.iv]
*Richard has ordered that the Lord Hastings be executed
before he dines*

Here's a good world the while! Who is so gross
That cannot see this palpable device?
Yet who so bold but says he sees it not? [III.vi]
*Everyone knows the evil that goes on, but none dare
denounce it*

Pity, you ancient stones, those tender babes
Whom envy hath immur'd within your walls,
Rough cradle for such little pretty ones.
Rude ragged nurse, old sullen playfellow
For tender princes, use my babies well. [IV.i]
Queen Elizabeth fears for the two princes in the Tower

'O, thus' quoth Dighton 'lay the gentle babes' –
'Thus, thus,' quoth Forrest 'girdling one another
Within their alabaster innocent arms.
Their lips were four red roses on a stalk,
And in their summer beauty kiss'd each other.
A book of prayers on their pillow lay;
Which once,' quoth Forrest 'almost chang'd my
mind.' [IV.iii]
*Tyrrel recounts the report of the two men who smothered
the princes in the Tower*

Thou cam'st on earth to make the earth my hell.
A grievous burden was thy birth to me;
Tetchy and wayward was thy infancy;
Thy school-days frightful, desp'rate, wild, and
furious;
Thy prime of manhood daring, bold, and venturous;
Thy age confirm'd, proud, subtle, sly, and bloody,
More mild, but yet more harmful-kind in hatred.
What comfortable hour canst thou name
That ever grac'd me with thy company? [IV.iv]
Richard's mother delivers a tirade against her evil son

My conscience hath a thousand several tongues,
And every tongue brings in a several tale,
And every tale condemns me for a villain.
[V.iii]
Richard is feeling pangs of guilt

I shall despair. There is no creature loves me;
And if I die no soul will pity me:
And wherefore should they, since that I myself
Find in myself no pity to myself? [V.iii]
Richard realises that he is completely unloved

By the apostle Paul, shadows to-night
Have struck more terror to the soul of Richard
Than can the substance of ten thousand soldiers.
[V.iii]
Richard has been terrified by a dream

Conscience is but a word that cowards use,
Devis'd at first to keep the strong in awe. [V.iii]
Richard, about to go into battle, has found his courage again

A horse! a horse! my kingdom for a horse! [V.iv]
Richard's horse has been killed beneath him

The day is ours, the bloody dog is dead. [V.v]
Richmond telling Derby that he has killed Richard

Now civil wounds are stopp'd, peace lives again –
That she may long live here, God say amen! [V.v]
Richmond marks the end of the years of civil war

Henry VIII

Written 1612-3

Time and place of action Early 16th-Century
England

*King Henry puts aside his wife, Katherine, in
favour of Anne Bullen. Cardinal Wolsey then falls
from favour when his attempts to prevent the re-
marriage are discovered, thus putting an end to a
career of self-serving arrogance. Queen Katherine
dies after the King has secretly married her sup-
planter. A plot against Cranmer, the new
Archbishop of Canterbury, is quashed by the King.
At the birth of Princess Elizabeth (Elizabeth I to
be) a prosperous future is foretold.*

Heat not a furnace for your foe so hot
That it do singe yourself. [I.i]
*Norfolk to Buckingham, advising him not to let his anger
with Wolsey carry him away*

Go with me like good angels to my end;
And as the long divorce of steel falls on me
Make of your prayers one sweet sacrifice,
And lift my soul to heaven. [II.i]
Buckingham, under guard, asks for his friends' prayers

Chamberlain: It seems the marriage with his
brother's wife
Has crept too near his conscience.
Suffolk: No, his conscience
Has crept too near another lady. [II.ii]
Suffolk is talking of the King's desire for Anne Bullen

I swear 'tis better to be lowly born
And range with humble livers in content
Than to be perk'd up in a glist'ring grief
And wear a golden sorrow. [II.iii]
*Anne Bullen says she prefers her happy, poor lot to that
of the Queen*

I shall fall
Like a bright exhalation in the evening,
And no man see me more. [III.ii]
Cardinal Wolsey realises his position is destroyed

Farewell, a long farewell, to all my greatness!
This is the state of man: to-day he puts forth
The tender leaves of hopes; to-morrow blossoms

And bears his blushing honours thick upon him;
The third day comes a frost, a killing frost,
And when he thinks, good easy man, full surely
His greatness is a-ripening, nips his root,
And then he falls, as I do. I have ventur'd,
Like little wanton boys that swim on bladders,
This many summers in a sea of glory;
But far beyond my depth. My high-blown pride
At length broke under me, and now has left me,
Weary and old with service, to the mercy
Of a rude stream, that must for ever hide me.
Vain pomp and glory of this world, I hate ye;
I feel my heart new open'd. O, how wretched
Is that poor man that hangs on princes' favours!
There is betwixt that smile we would aspire to,
That sweet aspect of princes, and their ruin
More pangs and fears than wars or women have;
And when he falls, he falls like Lucifer,
Never to hope again. [III.ii]
Wolsey soliloquising on his fate

Cromwell, I charge thee, fling away ambition:
By that sin fell the angels. How can man then,
The image of his Maker, hope to win by it?
Love thyself last; cherish those hearts that hate thee;
Corruption wins not more than honesty.
Still in thy right hand carry gentle peace
To silence envious tongues. Be just, and fear not;

Let all the ends thou aim'st at be thy country's,
Thy God's, and truth's; then, if thou fall'st, O
Cromwell,
Thou fall'st a blessed martyr! [III.ii]
Wolsey's advice to Cromwell

Had I but serv'd my God with half the zeal
I serv'd my King, he would not in mine age
Have left me naked to mine enemies. [III.ii]
Wolsey regrets not having served God so well as the King

So may he rest; his faults lie gently on him! [IV.ii]
Katherine forgives Wolsey

He was a scholar, and a ripe and good one;
Exceeding wise, fair-spoken, and persuading;
Lofty and sour to them that lov'd him not,
But to those men that sought him sweet as summer.
[IV.ii]
Griffith acknowledges that Wolsey was not all bad

Those about her
From her shall read the perfect ways of honour,
And by those claim their greatness not by blood.
Nor shall this peace sleep with her; but as when
The bird of wonder dies, the maiden phoenix,
Her ashes new create another heir
As great in admiration as herself. [V.v]
Cranmer talking of the future Queen Elizabeth

POEMS AND SONNETS

The Passionate Pilgrim

Crabbed age and youth cannot live together:
Youth is full of pleasance, age is full of care
Youth like summer brave, age like winter bare
Yout is full of sport, age's breath is short;
Youth is nimble, age is lame;
Youth is hot and bold, age is weak and cold;
Youth is wild, and age is tame.
Age, I do abhor thee; youth, I do adore thee
O, my love, my love is young!
Age, I do defy thee. [xii]

The Phoenix and the Turtle

Let the bird of loudest lay,
On the sole Arabian tree,
Herald sad and trumpet be,
To whose sound chaste wings obey. [1.i]

Venus and Adonis

The goddess of love becomes violently enamoured of the mortal youth, Adonis, and mourns him when he is slain while hunting the boar

If the first heire of my invention prove deformed, I shall be sorie it had so noble a god-father.
[Dedication]

Hunting he lov'd, but love he laugh'd to scorn. [1.iv]

Bid me discourse, I will enchant thine ear,
Or, like a fairy, trip upon the green,
Or, like a nymph, with long dishevelled hair,
Dance on the sands, and yet no footing seen.
Love is a spirit all compact of fire,
Not gross to sink, but light, and will aspire. [1.145]

Round-hoof'd, short-jointed, fetlocks shag and long,
Broad breast, full eye, small head, and nostril wide,
High crest, short ears, straight legs and passing strong,
Thin mane, thick tail, broad buttock, tender hide;
Look what a horse should have he did not lack,

Save a proud rider on so proud a back. [1.296]

If he did see his face, why then I know
He thought to kiss him, and hath kill'd him so.
"'Tis true, 'tis true; thus was Adonis slain. [1.1109]

The Rape of Lucrece

*Tarquin, Prince of Rome, ravishes the chaste Lucretia
and she kills herself to wipe away her shame*

Beauty itself doth of itself persuade
The eyes of men without an orator. [1.29]

Who buys a minute's mirth to wail a week?
Or sells eternity to get a toy?
For one sweet grape who will the vine destroy? [1.213]

Time's glory is to calm contending kings,
To unmask falsehood, and bring truth to light. [1.939]

And now this pale swan in her wat'ry nest
Begins the sad dirge of her certain ending. [1.1611]

Sonnets

Sonnets 1-126 chronicle an intense platonic love between the poet and a young man remarkable for his beauty. At first he tries to persuade the youth to perpetuate his beauty through marriage and children. Then, declaring his love, he vows to celebrate and immortalize his friend through poetry: time will destroy all things except this.

Sonnets 127-154 deal in more fragmented form with the poet's relations with his mistress – the so-called 'Dark lady' – through the poems may have been written at different times to different women.

From fairest creatures we desire increase,
That thereby beauty's rose might never die. [1]

When forty winters shall besiege thy brow,
And dig deep trenches in thy beauty's field. [2]

Thou art thy mother's glass, and she in thee
Calls back the lovely April of her prime. [3]

Music to hear, why hear'st thou music sadly?
Sweets with sweets war not, joy delights in joy.
Why lov'st thou that which thou receiv'st not gladly,
Or else receiv'st with pleasure thine annoy?
If the true concord of well-tuned sounds,
By unions married, do offend thine ear,
They do but sweetly chide thee. [8]

When do I count the clock that tells the time,
And see the brave day sunk in hideous night;
When I behold the violet past prime,
And sable curls all silver'd o'er with white;
When lofty trees I see barren of leaves,
Which erst from heat did canopy the herd,
And summer's green all girded up in sheaves
Borne on the bier with white and bristly beard;
Then of thy beauty do I question make
That thou among the wastes of time must go,
Since sweets and beauties do themselves forsake,
And die as fast as they see others grow;
And nothing 'gainst Time's scythe can make defence
Save breed, to brave him when he takes thee hence.
[12]

And all in war with Time for love of you!
As he takes from you, I engraft you new. [15]

If I could write the beauty of your eyes
And in fresh numbers number all your graces,
The age to come would say `This poet lies;
Such heavenly touches ne'er touch'd earthly faces'.
So should my papers, yellowed with their age,
Be scorn'd, like old men of less truth than tongue;
And your true rights be term'd a poet's rage,
And stretched metre of an antique song. [17]

Shall I compare thee to a summer's day?
Thou art more lovely and more temperate.
Rough winds do shake the darling buds of May,
And summer's lease hath all too short a date:
Sometime too hot the eye of heaven shines,
And often is his gold complexion dimm'd;
And every fair from fair some time declines,
By chance, or nature's changing course, untrimm'd;
But thy eternal summer shall not fade
Nor lose possession of that fair thou ow'st;
Nor shall Death brag thou wand'rest in his shade,
When in eternal lines to time thou grow'st.
So long as men can breathe or eyes can see,
So long lives this, and this gives life to thee. [18]

A woman's face, with Nature's own hand painted,
Hast thou, the Master Mistress of my passion. [20]

My glass shall not persuade me I am old
So long as youth and thou are of one date;
But when in thee time's furrows I behold,
Then look I death my days should expiate. [22]

O, let my looks be then the eloquence
And dumb presagers of my speaking breast. [23]

Mine eye hath play'd the painter and hath stell'd
Thy beauty's form in table of my heart. [24]

Weary with toil, I haste me to my bed,
The dear repose for limbs with travel tired;
But then begins a journey in my head
To work my mind when body's work's expired;
For then my thoughts, from far where I abide,
Intend a zealous pilgrimage to thee. [27]

When in disgrace with Fortune and men's eyes,
I all alone beweep my outcast state,

And trouble deaf heaven with my bootless cries,
And look upon myself, and curse my fate,
Wishing me like to one more rich in hope,
Featur'd like him, like him with friends possess'd,
Desiring this man's art, and that man's scope,
With what I most enjoy contented least;
Yet in these thoughts myself almost despising,
Haply I think on thee, and then my state,
Like to the lark at break of day arising
From sullen earth, sings hymns at heaven's gate;
For thy sweet love remember'd such wealth brings
That then I scorn to change my state with kings. [29]

When to the sessions of sweet silent thought
I summon up remembrance of things past,
I sigh the lack of many a thing I sought,
And with old woes new wail my dear time's waste.
Then can I drown an eye, unus'd to flow,
For precious friends hid in death's dateless night,
And weep afresh love's long since cancell'd woe,
And moan th' expense of many a vanish'd sight.
Then can I grieve at grievances foregone,
And heavily from woe to woe tell o'er
The sad account of fore-bemoaned moan,
Which I new pay as if not paid before.
But if the while I think on thee, dear friend,
All losses are restor'd, and sorrows end. [30]

Full many a glorious morning have I seen
Flatter the mountain-tops with sovereign eye,
Kissing with golden face the meadows green,
Gilding pale streams with heavenly alchemy ...

But out, alack! he was but one hour mine,
The region cloud hath mask'd him from me now.
Yet him for this my love no whit disdaineth;
Suns of the world may stain when heaven's sun
staineth. [33]

Why didst thou promise such a beauteous day,
And make me travel forth without my cloak,
To let base clouds o'ertake me in my way,
Hiding thy brav'ry in their rotten smoke? [34]

Roses have thorns, and silver fountains mud;
Clouds and eclipses stain both moon and sun,
And loathsome canker lives in sweetest bud.
All men make faults. [35]

Mine eye and heart are at a mortal war
How to divide the conquest of thy sight. [46]

Against that time when thou shalt strangely pass
And scarcely greet me with that sun, thine eye,
When love, converted from the thing it was,
Shall reasons find of settled gravity. [49]

Not marble nor the gilded monuments
Of princes shall outlive this pow'rful rhyme;
But you shall shine more bright in these contents
Than unswept stone, besmear'd with sluttish time.
[55]

Being your slave, what should I do but tend
Upon the hours and times of your desire?
I have no precious time at all to spend,
Nor services to do, till you require.
Nor dare I chide the world-without-end hour,
Whilst I, my sovereign, watch the clock for you,
Nor think the bitterness of absence sour,
When you have bid your servant once adieu;
Nor dare I question with my jealous thought
Where you may be, or your affairs suppose,
But, like a sad slave, stay and think of nought
Save where you are how happy you make those.
So true a fool is love that in your will,

Though you do anything, he thinks no ill. [57]

Like as the waves make towards the pebbled shore,
So do our minutes hasten to their end ...

Time doth transfix the flourish set on youth,
And delves the parallels in beauty's brow. [60]

Sin of self-love possesseth all mine eye,
And all my soul, and all my every part. [62]

When I have seen by Time's fell hand defaced
The rich proud cost of outworn buried age ...

When I have seen the hungry ocean gain
Advantage on the kingdom of the shore ...

This thought is as a death, which cannot choose
But weep to have that which it fears to lose. [64]

Since brass, nor stone, nor earth, nor boundless sea,
But sad mortality o'ersways their power,
How with this rage shall beauty hold a plea,
Whose action is no stronger than a flower? [65]

Tir'd with all these, for restful death I cry:
As, to behold desert a beggar born,
And needy nothing trimm'd in jollity,
And purest faith unhappily forsworn,
And gilded honour shamefully misplac'd,
And maiden virtue rudely strumpeted,
And right perfection wrongfully disgrac'd,
And strength by limping sway disabled,
And art made tongue-tied by authority,
And folly, doctor-like, controlling skill,
And simple truth miscall'd simplicity,
And captive good attending captain ill:
Tir'd with all these, from these would I be gone,
Save that, to die, I leave my love alone. [66]

Those parts of thee that the world's eye doth view
Want nothing that the thought of hearts can mend.
All tongues, the voice of souls, give thee that due,
Utt'ring bare truth, even so as foes commend. [69]

No longer mourn for me when I am dead
Than you shall hear the surly sullen bell
Give warning to the world that I am fled
From this vile world, with vilest worms to dwell. [71]

That time of year thou mayst in me behold
When yellow leaves, or none, or few, do hang
Upon those boughs which shake against the cold,
Bare ruin'd choirs where late the sweet birds sang.
In me thou seest the twilight of such day
As after sunset fadeth in the west,
Which by and by black night doth take away,
Death's second self, that seals up all in rest. [73]

O, know, sweet love, I always write of you,
And you and love are still my argument;
So all my best is dressing old words new,
Spending again what is already spent. [76]

Time's thievish progress to eternity. [77]

Your monument shall be my gentle verse,
Which eyes not yet created shall o'er-read;
And tongues to be your being shall rehearse,
When all the breathers of this world are dead.
You still shall live, such virtue hath my pen,
Where breath most breathes, even in the mouths of
men. [81]

Was it the proud full sail of his great verse,
Bound for the prize of all-too-precious you,
That did my ripe thoughts in my brain inhearse,
Making their tomb the womb wherein they grew?
[86]

Farewell! thou art too dear for my possessing,
And like enough thou know'st thy estimate.
The charter of thy worth gives thee releasing;
My bonds in thee are all determinate.
For how do I hold thee but by thy granting?
And for that riches where is my deserving?
The cause of this fair gift in me is wanting,
And so my patent back again is swerving.
Thyself thou gav'st, thy own worth then not know-
ing,
Or me, to whom thou gav'st it, else mistaking;
So thy great gift, upon misprision growing,
Comes home again, on better judgment making.
Thus have I had thee, as a dream doth flatter:
In sleep a king, but, waking, no such matter. [87]

For thee, against myself I'll vow debate,
For I must ne'er love him whom thou dost hate. [89]

Ah, do not, when my heart hath scap'd this sorrow,
Come in the rearward of a conquer'd woe;
Give not a windy night a rainy morrow,
To linger out a purpos'd overthrow. [90]

They that have power to hurt and will do none,
That do not do the thing they most do show,
Who, moving others, are themselves as stone,
Unmoved, cold, and to temptation slow;
They rightly do inherit Heaven's graces,
And husband nature's riches from expense;
They are the lords and owners of their faces,
Others but stewards of their excellence.
The summer's flow'r is to the summer sweet
Though to itself it only live and die;
But if that flow'r with base infection meet,
The basest weed outbraves his dignity.
For sweetest things turn sourest by their deeds;
Lilies that fester smell far worse than weeds. [94]

How like a winter hath my absence been
From thee, the pleasure of the fleeting year!
What freezings have I felt, what dark days seen!
What old December's bareness everywhere! [97]

From you have I been absent in the spring,
When proud-pied April, dress'd in all his trim,
Hath put a spirit of youth in every thing. [98]

O truant Muse, what shall be thy amends
For thy neglect of truth in beauty dy'd?
Both truth and beauty on my love depends;
So dost thou too, and therein dignified. [101]

For to no other pass my verses tend
Than of your graces and your gifts to tell;
And more, much more, than in my verse can sit
Your own glass shows you, when you look in it.
[103]

To me, fair friend, you never can be old,
For as you were when first your eye I ey'd,
Such seems your beauty still. Three winters cold
Have from the forests shook three summers' pride,
Three beauteous springs to yellow autumn turn'd
In process of the seasons have I seen,
Three April perfumes in three hot Junes burn'd,
Since first I saw you fresh, which yet are green.
Ah, yet doth beauty, like a dial-hand,

Steal from his figure, and no pace perceiv'd;
So your sweet hue, which methinks still doth stand,
Hath motion, and mine eye may be deceiv'd.
For fear of which, hear this, thou age unbred:
Ere you were born was beauty's summer dead.
[104]

Fair, kind, and true, have often liv'd alone,
Which three, till now, never kept seat in one. [105]

When in the chronicle of wasted time
I see descriptions of the fairest wights,
And beauty making beautiful old rhyme,
In praise of ladies dead and lovely knights ...

For we, which now behold these present days,
Have eyes to wonder, but lack tongues to praise.
[106]

Not mine own fears, nor the prophetic soul
Of the wide world dreaming on things to come,
Can yet the lease of my true love control,
Suppos'd as forfeit to a confin'd doom.
The mortal moon hath her eclipse endur'd,
And the sad augurs mock their own presage ...

And thou in this shalt find thy monument,
When tyrants' crests and tombs of brass are spent.
[107]

Alas, 'tis true I have gone here and there
And made myself a motley to the view,
Gor'd mine own thoughts, sold cheap what is most-
dear,
Made old offences of affections new.
Most true it is that I have look'd on truth
Askance and strangely; but, by all above,
These blenches gave my heart another youth,
And worse essays prov'd thee my best of love. [110]

Let me not to the marriage of true minds
Admit impediments. Love is not love
Which alters when it alteration finds,
Or bends with the remover to remove.
O, no! it is an ever-fixed mark,
That looks on tempests and is never shaken;
It is the star to every wand'ring bark,
Whose worth's unknown, although his height be
taken.
Love's not Time's fool, though rosy lips and cheeks
Within his bending sickle's compass come;
Love alters not with his brief hours and weeks,

But bears it out even to the edge of doom.
If this be error, and upon me prov'd,
I never writ, nor no man ever lov'd. [116]

What potions have I drunk of Siren tears,
Distill'd from limbecks foul as hell within,
Applying fears to hopes, and hopes to fears,
Still losing when I saw myself to win! [119]

'Tis better to be vile than vile esteemed,
When not to be receives reproach of being,
And the just pleasure lost, which is so deemed
Not by our feeling, but by others' seeing. [121]

No, Time, thou shalt no boast that I do change.
Thy pyramids built up with newer might
To me are nothing novel, nothing strange;
They are but dressings of a former sight. [123]

The' expense of spirit in a waste of shame
Is lust in action; and till action, lust
Is perjur'd, murd'rous, bloody, full of blame,
Savage, extreme, rude, cruel, not to trust,

283

Enjoyed no sooner but despised straight;
Past reason hunted; and no sooner had,
Past reason hated, as a swallowed bait,
On purpose laid to make the taker mad –
Mad in pursuit, and in possession so;
Had, having, and in quest to have, extreme;
A bliss in proof, and prov'd, a very woe;
Before, a joy propos'd; behind, a dream.
All this the world well knows; yet none knows well
To shun the heaven that leads men to this hell. [129]

My mistress' eyes are nothing like the sun;
Coral is far more red than her lips' red;
If snow be white, why then her breasts are dun;
If hairs be wires, black wires grow on her head.
I have seen roses damask'd, red and white,
But no such roses see I in her cheeks;
And in some perfumes is there more delight
Than in the break that from my mistress reeks.
I love to hear her speak, yet well I know
That music hath a far more pleasing sound;
I grant I never saw a goddess go –
My mistress when she walks treads on the ground.
And yet, by heaven, I think my love as rare
As any she belied with false compare. [130]

Make but my name thy love, and love that still,
And then thou lov'st me, for my name is Will. [136]

Thou blind fool, Love, what dost thou to mine eyes
That they behold, and see not what they see? [137]

When my love swears that she is made of truth,
I do believe her, though I know she lies. [138]

Two loves I have, of comfort and despair,
Which like two spirits do suggest me still:
The better angel is a man right fair,
The worser spirit a woman colour'd ill. [144]

Poor soul, the centre of my sinful earth,
[My sinful earth] these rebel pow'rs that thee array,
Why dost thou pine within and suffer dearth,
Painting thy outward walls so costly gay?
Why so large cost, having so short a lease,
Dost thou upon thy fading mansion spend? ...

So shalt thou feed on Death, that feeds on men,
And, Death once dead, there's no more dying then.
[146]

Past cure I am, now reason is past care,
And frantic mad with evermore unrest;
My thoughts and my discourse as mad men's are,
At random from the truth vainly express'd;
For I have sworn thee fair, and thought thee bright,
Who art as black as hell, as dark as night. [147]

For I have sworn thee fair – more perjur'd I,
To swear against the truth so foul a lie! [152]

Love's fire heats water, water cools not love. [154]

Good friend, for Jesus' sake forbear,
To dig the dust enclosed here!
Blest be the man that spares these stones
And curst be he that moves my bones. [Epitaph]

Item, I give unto my wife my second best bed. [Will]

COLLINS CLASSICS

Complete Novels of Jane Austen
With introductions by Patrick O'Brian, Reginald Hill
and others

Complete Novels of Charlotte & Emily Brontë
With introductions by Hilary Mantel, Robert
Barnard and others

Complete Works of Shakespeare
With introductions by Germaine Greer, Anthony
Burgess and others

Complete Works of Oscar Wilde
With introductions by Vyvyan Holland, Merlin
Holland and others

*Complete Sherlock Holmes & Other Detective
Stories by Sir Arthur Conan Doyle*
With introduction by Owen Dudley Edwards

Complete Novels of Thomas Hardy
With introduction by Roy Hattersley

COLLINS GEM

Bestselling Collins Gem titles include:

Gem English Dictionary (£3.50)

Gem Calorie Counter (£2.99)

Gem Thesaurus (£2.99)

Gem French Dictionary (£3.50)

Gem German Dictionary (£3.50)

Gem Burns Anthology (£3.50)

Gem Birds (£3.50)

Gem Babies' Names (£3.50)

Gem Card Games (£3.50)

Gem World Atlas (£3.50)

All Collins Gems are available from your local bookseller or can be ordered direct from the publishers.

In the UK, contact Mail Order, Dept 2M, HarperCollins Publishers, Westerhill Rd, Bishopbriggs, Glasgow, G64 2QT, listing the titles required and enclosing a cheque or p.o. for the value of the books plus £1.00 for the first title and 25p for each additional title to cover p&p. Access and Visa cardholders can order on 041-772 2281 (24 hr).

In Australia, contact Customer Services, HarperCollins Distribution, Yarrawa Rd, Moss Vale 2577 (tel. [048] 68 0300). **In New Zealand**, contact Customer Services, HarperCollins Publishers, 31 View Rd, Glenfield, Auckland 10 (tel. [09] 444 3740). **In Canada**, contact your local bookshop.

All prices quoted are correct at time of going to press.